Nothing But the Truth

Essays in Apologetics

KARL KEATING

Nothing But
the Truth

Essays in Apologetics

CATHOLIC ANSWERS
SAN DIEGO
1999

Published by Catholic Answers, Inc.
2020 Gillespie Way
El Cajon, California 92020
(888) 291-8000 (orders)
(619) 387-0042 (fax)
www.catholic.com (web)
Cover design by Claudine Guerguerian
Printed in the United States of America
ISBN 1-888992-12-3

Contents

For my parents,
who taught me that truth matters

Preface

James Boswell described to Samuel Johnson an "impudent fellow" who "railed at all established systems." The man "maintained that there was no distinction between virtue and vice."

"Why, Sir," responded Johnson, "if the fellow does not think as he speaks, he is lying; and I see not what honour he can propose to himself from having the character of a lyar. But if he does really think that there is no distinction between virtue and vice, why, Sir, when he leaves our houses let us count our spoons."

Some "impudent fellows" steal flatware, which is bad enough. Others, not distinguishing between intellectual virtue and vice, obscure or even oppose the truth, which is worse. They may be found at all parts of the spectrum—left and right, inside the Church and outside. Each of these essays reveals the ideas and temperament of such people, either directly or, in two or three cases, by way of a display of opposite qualities.

I hope these pages will comfort those who, knowing truth matters, sometimes become discouraged when so many around them seem uninterested in truth.

I

When Not to Turn the Other Cheek

Those who take public stands open themselves to public abuse. Ask any apologist. If the abuse comes from the unlettered or unmannered, the apologist sloughs it off. But if the abuse comes from someone who in other contexts seems the epitome of intelligence and courtesy, the barbs sting. In that case one's first instinct is defense, to salvage one's reputation.

After a few moments comes the realization that perhaps even these barbs should go unremarked—better to say nothing, let the matter pass. Further consideration brings nagging questions: What if more than my own reputation is at stake? What if, by keeping silent, I allow the faith to be tarnished and people to be scandalized? On the other hand, is my desire to vindicate the faith masking a deeper desire to vindicate myself? Is my pride overpowering prudence, or is it pride that encourages me to sit out the fray?

These are questions that assail anyone who is attacked in public. Some people are paralyzed by them, unable to find answers. Others perceive their duty at once and act. So it was with John Henry Newman. When he converted from Anglicanism to Catholicism in 1845, Newman lost not just his living but most of his friends. His conversion was perceived by many not as a change of heart or mind but as a moral lapse. The press attacked him with vigor. The reestablishment of the Catholic hierarchy in 1850 induced a new outbreak of anti-Catholic sentiment; though not then attacked personally, Newman took up his pen in defense of the Church. Once the fever of bigotry cooled, his name was no longer on everyone's tongue. There followed for him years of relative calm, but that suddenly changed in 1864.

The January issue of *Macmillan's Magazine* included a review of the seventh and eighth volumes of J. A. Froude's *History of England*. The review was signed only with the initials "C. K." The identity of the reviewer might have remained unknown to the general public if he had not included several lines that were to ensure his lasting notoriety. Were it not for thirty words, Charles Kingsley—professor of history at Cambridge, popular novelist, opponent of the Oxford Movement, and anti-Catholic—would be known today only by specialists in Victorian studies. He had the personal misfortune (for us, a *felix culpa*) of penning words that were to result in the greatest work of its kind since Augustine's *Confessions*, Newman's *Apologia Pro Vita Sua*. Kingsley imprudently wrote, "Truth, for its own sake, has never been a virtue with the Roman clergy. Father Newman informs us that it need not, and on the whole ought not to be." He had brought up Newman's name almost as an aside. It proved to be a major blunder.

There ensued a correspondence between Kingsley and Newman, an exchange eventually reproduced in the *Apologia*. Newman undoubtedly had the better of it. However skilled as a writer, Kingsley was outclassed by his adversary. When Newman converted, in 1845, the whole of England seemed against him, but his *Essay on the Development of Christian Doctrine*, completed as he converted, could not be dismissed lightly. Five years later the Catholic hierarchy was reestablished in Britain. Protestant opponents termed it the "Papal Aggression," and popular anti-Catholic bigotry reached new highs (and lows). Defending the Church in a series of lectures (published in 1851 as *The Present Position of Catholics in England*), Newman used high satire to ridicule popular bigotry. He later would call the book one of only three he deemed "controversial," the others being his *Difficulties of Anglicans* and, of all things, one of his two novels, *Loss and Gain*.

In answer to Kingsley's charges, Newman wrote the "history of his religious opinions," as he subtitled the *Apologia*, between April 21 and June 2, 1864. One part appeared each Thursday. "The success of the *Apologia* was instantaneous," said Anton Pegis a century later, "and that is a remarkable fact, and also a remarkable tribute to Newman, when we remember the unpopularity of the Catholic cause in England. Long after he had crushed Kingsley, Newman captured the English world by the clear and impassioned honesty of the personal history which he bared to public gaze." Through that personal defense Newman succeeded in defending the Catholic faith.

In an enlarged preface for the final edition of 1873, Newman briefly recounted the quarrel, without mentioning his opponent by name. On seeing Kingsley's pamphlet,

> I recognized what I had to do, though I shrank from both the task and the exposure which it would entail. I must, I said, give the true key to my whole life; I must show what I am, that it may be seen what I am not, and that the phantom may be extinguished which gibbers instead of me. I wish to be known as a living man, and not as a scarecrow which is dressed up in my clothes. False ideas may be refuted indeed by argument, but by true ideas alone are they expelled.

This passage, read in isolation, might lead one to think Newman, not wanting to be seen as a "gibbering phantom," was worried only about his reputation, but the context of his remarks demonstrates a larger concern. Kingsley was attacking not so much Newman as the Catholic priesthood. The Anglican novelist subscribed to the notion that every priest was "jesuitical," in the worst sense of that term. To slander Newman was to slander the priesthood—and thus the whole Church.

What was the proper response for Newman? Kingsley had not been the first to criticize him, and Newman generally ignored criticisms or commented on them only in private correspondence. This time it was different. A respected and influential man of letters had insulted the priesthood of the Catholic Church by insulting Newman, and a defense of the priesthood, if it were to come from Newman, had to be in terms of a defense of Newman himself.

"To him who strikes you on the cheek, offer the other also," our Lord admonished (Luke 5:29). Yet the same Lord cleansed the Temple when his Father's house suffered desecration by the moneychangers. It is one thing to permit, in silence, the sullying of one's own reputation. It is something else to keep silent and out of harm's way when the reputation of the Church is at stake. In weighing whether to respond to Kingsley, Newman no doubt pondered Ecclesiastes 3:7: There is "a time to keep silence, and a time to speak." For him, it was time to speak.

The same dilemma confronts lesser men. Permit me an indulgence here, as I refer to a situation that occurred several years ago. I learned that a Catholic speaker—I will call him Z—had given a lecture at a prominent parish in Manhattan. The lecture itself did not interest me, but the question-and-answer session that followed it did: Nearly all of the session was a condemnation of me in particular and my apostolate, Catholic Answers, in general.

Obtaining a tape of the event, I called other staffers into my office, and we listened. The first question was posed by Z's friend (he did not identify himself, but we recognized his voice). His question was an example of what used to be known, in Marxist countries, as "planned spontaneity"—in other words, heavy-handed collusion. Was there anything Z wanted to say about those Catholics he perceived as in some way opposed to him? Why, yes, there was, Z said. His "answer" to the "question" lasted half a hour.

We marveled at the alacrity with which he took an event unrelated to himself, such as an employee's leaving Catholic Answers, and transformed it into an indictment: The employee must have left because he no longer could conscience Catholic Answers' "campaign" against Z. Did Z find that some of his speaking engagements didn't pan out? Then there must have been a Catholic Answers "conspiracy" against him. The acme was reached when he discussed "Celebrity Quotation Impersonated," a regular feature in *This Rock*, our monthly magazine. At the time of Z's lecture, we had been running the feature for well over two years. Each month we featured a "celebrity" from the past—maybe a Catholic (Mother Cabrini, Hernan Cortes), maybe a Protestant (Martin Luther, William Jennings Bryan), maybe someone less categorizable (Thomas Edison, Boss Tweed). Each "celebrity" gave an encomium for *This Rock*—all very tongue-in-cheek. Knowing that even the most dastardly man can have a deathbed conversion, we did not identify any celebrity's current location (except in the case of canonized saints, of course). This did not sit well with Z. He complained that the monthly spoof implied that "wild West outlaws" (he seemed to have in mind Buffalo Bill Cody) and Christian Scientists (one of the celebrities was Mary Baker Eddy) were in heaven. But that wasn't the worst part. He said he "sensed" that the staff of Catholic Answers had been running "Celebrity Quotation Impersonated" precisely to "annoy" *him*.

And so the tape recording went, half an hour of non sequiturs and embarrassments. What to do about it? How to respond? Whether to respond at all? The tape was marketed by a New Jersey-based organization that distributes some good Catholic material but also a noticeable percentage of kooky items. It advertises in publications read by Catholic Answers' supporters. They would see the ad for this tape and might purchase it; we worried what their reaction would be. As it turned out, we needn't have worried. The tape must not have sold widely—the ads ran for only a few issues, then disappeared—and we received only a handful of calls or letters.

But I didn't know that when I first heard Z's remarks. Tempted to blast him publicly, I decided to say nothing, except that I wrote to the pastor of the Manhattan parish because he is a prominent cleric, as are two priests in residence there, one a widely-known and articulate speaker (a convert from Anglicanism), the other Z's host. I told the pastor that I was "disappointed" to learn that Z had spoken at the parish, and, I said, I didn't want the pastor to think, through my silence, that I put any stock in Z's malevolent remarks. I sent photocopies of my letter to the two resident priests. From Z's host I heard nothing. From the convert/speaker I received a kind and understanding telephone call. From the pastor I received a rude note. He mistakenly thought I blamed *him* for Z's remarks. My "Heads up!" had turned to bite me, proving again that, among lesser apologists, no attempt at self-exculpation goes unpunished.

If Newman and I share any trait, it is defensiveness. I think this trait is found in most apologists, whether they engage in apologetics as a vocation or merely as an avocation. Rare is the man who takes no umbrage when being assailed unjustly, who feels no anger when his most-cherished beliefs are attacked and his name besmirched. Defensiveness in such circumstances may not be commendable, but it is understandable among the fallen sons of Adam. That said, how is one to move beyond this feeling of defensiveness? How does one decide when to "turn the other cheek" and when it is "a time to speak"? This is a matter of prudential judgment, I think, so there can be no hard-and-fast rule, no mathematical formula into which one stuffs data and out of which is spit an infallible answer.

Part of the measure must be the extent of the perceived injury. Is it limited to my own reputation? Then it is ignorable and should be ignored, there being too much danger of escalation: "Did so! Did not! *Ka-boom!*" A private disappointment could be turned into a public disgrace. Thus I refrained from publicly responding to Z. (I should have gone further and skipped the letter to the pastor —my defensiveness got the better of me.) But if the injury extends past the individual and to a wider audience—innocents who might be misled, scandal arising from silence, the faith itself called into question—then it ceases to be a matter of self-defense and becomes the defense of third parties. The apologist has a positive duty to respond, as Newman had a duty to respond to Kingsley, even if, in doing so, he necessarily defended himself.

As on the battlefield, the attack defines the defense.

2

Answering an Absolutist

Dear Mr. L:

I suppose we look at things through different spectacles.

You think I fail because Protestant controversialists agree to debate me publicly. If I were doing things right, you say, they'd run away from me, as they run away from you. Your conclusion is that your arguments are impossible for them to refute so they wisely keep their distance, but mine are second-rate so they readily take me on. I admit my arguments may be second-rate. I'll go further and confess they aren't even mine. There isn't a one, I think, that I haven't borrowed from someone like Frank Sheed or Arnold Lunn or John Henry Newman, not to mention from Augustine and Thomas Aquinas. But what do I know? Maybe such men preferred second-rate arguments.

I can't help thinking, though, that Protestants may decline to debate you for reasons other than the solidity of your arguments. They might be running away from you because of your attitude toward them, especially the ex-Catholics. You seem to think a Catholic becomes a Protestant because he consciously embraces sin and for no other reason. Granted, sin at times plays a part, but I suspect it usually doesn't play the leading role—or the solitary role—you assign it.

Can I explain fully why people leave the Church and adhere to another religion? No, and I can't explain fully why they come back. Ultimately it is a matter of grace and therefore of mystery. What I am engaged in, apologetics, is at a lower level. Apologetics is the reasoned defense of the faith, and its tool is the argument. No one ever became a Catholic or returned to the Catholic faith by argument alone. The most an argument can do is clear the path so there aren't as many stumbling blocks to accepting the grace God offers. (This is what the old texts called "the motives of credibility.")

Faith is a gift, and it's a gift that's freely accepted or freely rejected. That granted, it still isn't easy to see the whys and wherefores; our fallen nature confuses our motives and clouds our sense. We must admit that in any conversion, in any direction, there are many contributing factors, not just one. You are too reductionistic in saying that anyone who leaves the Church worships his own stomach instead of God, period. I don't think the empirical evidence backs that up. At the very least, conversions aren't (except in rare cases, perhaps) as cut and dried as you think.

You say that "every person who 'leaves' the Church was never 'in' it." This is a dangerous argument. It's dangerous because it implies we never can know whether a man is a Catholic until he's safely dead. One consequence is that we never can know who's a priest (a man first must qualify as a real Catholic, of course) and who isn't. But the Church has never accepted this line of thought, which is reminiscent of Donatism.

A baptized infant is a Catholic, even though he can't make an act of faith. A man who falls away from the practice of his religion through laziness but doesn't subscribe to another remains a Catholic. He's a lapsed Catholic but still a Catholic. It's only when he rejects Catholicism for another faith (or for no faith at all) that he ceases to be a Catholic.

In your own way, you have adopted Fundamentalism's notion of an absolute assurance of salvation. Fundamentalism, or at least the majority faction within it, says that someone who is "born again" can never lose salvation, no matter what sins he might commit later. You say something analogous. You say a real Catholic never will fall away from the Church, no matter what, but that can be true, I suspect, only if we narrow the definition of Catholic and adopt a private definition of the term. (Remember that even the apostle Paul worried about losing the faith—and who, after what happened on the Damascus Road, could have been more authentically Catholic?)

Now I'll admit conversions away from the faith can involve sin.

It's easy enough to point to some professional anti-Catholics, for example, who seem to have left Catholicism because they couldn't live up to its moral strictures and who "cover" their failings by attacking the Church. (In saying this about such men I am drawing a conclusion which I think is reasonable, based on evidence available to me, but I don't want to be absolutist here. I'm not a confessor and make no claim about reading souls. I'm speaking only of what seem to be probabilities and only of a few cases fairly well known to me. In these cases I conclude conversion had more to do with moral than with intellectual problems.)

However true this may be, however many people—professional anti-Catholics or otherwise—have left the Church due to sin, I don't think it's right to conclude everyone leaves for that reason alone or even that they leave primarily because of sin and only secondarily for other reasons. I know too many people who left precisely because they were seeking to escape sins in which they were embroiled.

They may have been Mass-going Catholic fornicators who became disgusted with their fornication and thought they found a better moral code in Fundamentalism, where they ceased fornicating. They might have been rosary-praying drunkards who found in Fundamentalism the strength to give up the bottle. In other words, conversion coincided with a net moral improvement. This isn't to say the improvement couldn't have come within Catholicism. The fact is that for these people it didn't.

In other cases, perhaps the majority, converts' moral lives seem unchanged by conversion. They lived as well before (so far as it's possible for us to know) as after. They converted not so much to escape or embrace sin, but for doctrinal reasons. They could find no answers to the questions put to them by non-Catholics, and they concluded—incorrectly, yes, but innocently, I think—that the religion of their upbringing was wrong and this other religion right.

It seems you are unwilling to allow ignorance much room. People are either knowledgeable Catholics, which means they never can be swayed by arguments put to them by Fundamentalists, or they aren't Catholics at all. Real life, I think, suggests otherwise.

Most Catholics aren't especially knowledgeable about their faith, and they will go wherever sense seems to lead them. This is nothing new.

Recall what happened to England at the time of the Reformation. When the government changed the official religion, some folks went into rebellion in order to defend Catholicism, but most didn't. Most swallowed what was offered them—some because they couldn't tell the difference, others because they didn't care. The majority of the English people went over to the new religion with little fuss. Yet before the Reformation would anyone deny these were Catholics? Uninstructed Catholics, yes, but Catholics still.

I must disagree with you when you say that the rejection of Catholicism is never done in good faith. If your comment is taken literally, it means that everyone who rejects Catholicism knows full well he's rejecting the true religion, but he does it anyway because he's caught in sin. I don't see how your principles can be applied in practice, especially to people who leave Catholicism precisely because they're seeking a deeper relationship with Christ. Yes, I admit they're mistaken to make the switch since what they're looking for, in its highest form, is right before them, not over yonder, but the fact remains that they are switching in good faith.

Don't get me wrong. I'm not condoning the switch, and I'm not denying the role of sin, in particular cases, nor the interest Screwtape's boss has in all this. And I'm not reducing everything to "psychological tendencies, lack of fellowship, or boring priests" (your words). In fact, if you had read my writings with any diligence, you'd know that I have emphasized, again and again, that these "emotional" factors are not what keep former Catholics in Fundamentalism. What keeps them there is doctrine. (Again, I don't deny there can be moral problems that play a part in keeping one away from Rome.)

Let me go back to your point about debates. You say I fail whenever a Protestant agrees to debate me. I suppose you also think I fail whenever one agrees to speak with me in private or when one corresponds with me. Well, if that's failure, let's have more of it, because it's only through such failure that misconceptions about the Catholic faith will be overcome.

You say, "All liars *fear* truth," which is true, but not all non-Catholics are liars. (Yes, yes: We're all liars at one time or another, but you mean by liars people who are consistently such, so I'll use the term the same way.) If you think everyone who disagrees with you on religion is a liar, and that seems to be a necessary conclusion from your premises, then you may be the only truth-teller in the world—perhaps I should say, in *your* world—since you will find most Catholics disagreeing with you in your assessment of what prompts conversions.

You end the body of your letter by insisting I rely too much on my own skills and not enough on God. You say I need help. "Feel free to call on me—when you realize that you need it." I admit I rely too much on myself and not enough on God. Believe me, I'm far more aware of my failings in this regard than you are. But I was surprised by your advice. As I read along, I thought you'd say, "Rely on God more." Instead you say I should call you.

Thanks, but I'll struggle along as I have. There's much I have to learn, and I've taken many wrong turns in this apostolate already. I'm convinced I've also taken a few right ones (thanks largely to ideas filched from the men named in my second paragraph). You will understand, I hope, when I say I'm not altogether convinced your understanding of apologetics is superior to mine. After all, you say you've questioned or debated dozens of Protestants, and they've told you that "sinning keeps one alive forever," that "heaven is a place of endless torment and punishment," that "God is a liar."

I don't know whom you spoke with, but I never met a Protestant who claimed anything like that, and I'm sure I've spoken to more Protestants than you have. I never even met a pagan who said such dumb things. And I doubt you have. If you understood Protestants to say such things, you entirely misconstrued their points, which suggests you may have misconstrued what makes people convert.

Thanks, but no thanks. I decline to conclude that everyone who makes an unwise change intends to abandon God.

3

What Does Father Mean?

The writers' adage has it that a bad review is better than no review. A critic may not like what has been written, but his taking notice is a sign that the text has at least some importance. I'm pleased to say that nearly all the reviews of *Pillar of Fire, Pillar of Truth*—a 32-page booklet distributed in the millions by Catholic Answers—have been complimentary, but a particular "pan" of the booklet intrigued me. It was written by a priest in Cleveland Heights, Ohio, and it appeared in his parish bulletin under the title "From the Pastor's Desk." I will call the priest Fr. M.

I reproduce his commentary in full, not so much because it demands a response (who outside the parish is likely ever to see it; who inside the parish even now remembers it?), but because his words aptly illustrate the way orthodox publications can have a cloud cast over them. Admittedly, I have a keen interest in his review because its subject is a booklet I helped to write, yet I think I am able to comment with a certain disinterestedness—but that's for the reader to decide.

Paragraphs in italic type are by Fr. M. My comments appear in roman type.

Recently, a brightly colored little booklet entitled Pillar of Fire, Pillar of Truth *has appeared at the church doors. It is not there with any official approbation, and no one has ever come forward and accepted responsibility for it or asked permission to distribute it.*

The first thing Fr. M does is cast suspicion on the booklet, which has "appeared" in his parish without "official approbation." This probably means that no one asked him if the booklet could be distributed in the church racks, but the word "official" suggests that a higher authority's sanction must be obtained to display literature—not true, of course.

The next phrase is one that might come from a prosecutor or a schoolmarm: "no one has ever come forward and accepted responsibility for it." You already know the writer has prejudged the matter. His choice of words betrays his thinking. Why not say instead, "No one has taken credit for putting the booklet in the racks" or "It is unknown who placed the booklet in the racks"? The former sentence has a slightly positive cast, the latter has a neutral cast, while Fr. M's has a decidedly negative cast.

Only with the issue of permission, I think, has Fr. M hit upon a valid complaint. Permission should have been asked first—unless the parish has a policy of allowing any non-offensive Catholic literature to be displayed. A few parishes take this approach and have become havens for second-hand literature.

I personally think that the booklet is not very endorsable and it would be better not distributed. The reason being that as a string of declarative sentences it is probably right, but when all the sentences are put together, you are left with declaration, tone, attitude, and questions about what has been left unsaid.

Is something wrong with declarative sentences? If so, Fr. M—in a commentary constructed out of declarative sentences—doesn't say. At least he says that each sentence, standing on its own, is "probably right," a welcome admission and nearly unavoidable, since *Pillar of Fire, Pillar of Truth* deals only with simple, verifiable facts and principles, most of which are taken straight from Scripture.

Then comes the curious part. Fr. M says that the whole is contrary to the sum of the individual parts. The individual sentences are correct, but when they are combined a cloud descends. You end up with "declaration" (which is what you might expect from declarative sentences), "tone, attitude" (code words—the "tone" or "attitude" of the booklet is that truth exists and can be known with certainty), "questions about what has been left unsaid." This last phrase needs examination. Is he referring to things left unsaid about the topics discussed in the booklet—the structure of the Church, the marks by which it can be identified, the papacy and episcopacy, the sacraments, Mary and the saints, salvation? If so, then the writers plead guilty.

In *Catholicism and Fundamentalism* I devoted thirty-four dense pages to the papacy and admittedly gave only an overview. *Pillar of Fire, Pillar of Truth* gives a little more than a page to the papacy —a page that contains perhaps half as many words as does a page of a book—so it's manifestly true that the booklet leaves much unsaid on each topic. But that's the right approach for an introductory work intended to pique the interest of the reader, to get him interested in the Catholic faith by highlighting a few of its major tenets. Do we complain about a table of contents because it doesn't approach the length of the main text?

I digress. It's likely that Fr. M isn't complaining that the booklet doesn't say enough about the topics it addresses. What he means is that he doesn't like the selection of topics. This becomes clear later.

Pillar of Fire, Pillar of Truth *is fairly antagonistic toward the "Bible churches," though it never defines which churches are included in this grouping. Many non-Catholic children who belong to Bible churches attend our school. A book like this does nothing to foster healthy understanding or inter-faith discussion. Its tone is also fairly anti-ecumenical and triumphalistic, and both of these attitudes have been rejected by the world-wide gathering of bishops in union with the Holy Father during the Vatican Council.*

Notice that Fr. M cites not one example of antagonism toward other churches. The closest the booklet comes to "antagonism" is to note that "many of the churches to which door-to-door missionaries belong" (most missionaries are Fundamentalists, Evangelicals, Mormons, or Jehovah's Witnesses) "began as recently as the nineteenth or twentieth centuries," and it says that the Catholic Church claims to have existed since the first century. All this is factual, isn't it?

It's laudable that "many non-Catholic children who belong to Bible churches" are enrolled in the parish school. I hope Fr. M is not so concerned about "upsetting" their parents that his school has shelved a clear explication of the Catholic faith. If it hasn't, then the booklet won't surprise anyone. If it has, then the booklet might be the ideal vehicle through which to teach the faith to the Catholic children (they need to know their own faith if they're to live as Catholics), while at the same time giving the non-Catholic children a view of Catholicism from the inside. How can there be "healthy understanding or inter-faith discussion" if Catholics can't explain their own faith and if non-Catholics, because of a misplaced fear of offending them, have not had it presented to them plainly? Ironically, the booklet's tone, which Fr. M terms "fairly anti-ecumenical," has been praised by many Protestants for being precisely the opposite—the tone fosters authentic ecumenism by giving the facts about Catholicism.

The thesis lacks a certain intellectual honesty because it never presents the Church as "sinful community" as being responsible for some of the problems in the area of credibility that the Church has to face.

I don't know what prompted this outburst about the Church being a "sinful community." Perhaps it was the section on holiness as one of the four identifying marks of the Church. The booklet shows why holiness is a signpost to the Church Jesus founded. A few pages on it explains briefly the role of sin in our lives and why Jesus gave us the gift of the sacrament of penance. This is an upbeat view. Fr. M seems to desire a negative view.

Finally, the use of Scripture is only probative and it is never used as a source of living faith or revelation of the Father's love. The knowledge of Christ does not appear to be expected to be relational but only observant. The Roman Catholic Church teaches that concern for justice is a consti-

tutive element of our faith; this little pamphlet never mentions justice at all.

Does *Pillar of Fire, Pillar of Truth* use Scripture in a "probative" manner? Of course. It uses Scripture to prove what it is asserting. Since all twenty-one ecumenical councils have done the same, and since Jesus quoted the Old Testament in a "probative" manner to establish his credentials, this use has a good pedigree.

Fr. M claims the booklet refers to rules but not to a relationship with God. Yet the third from the last section is titled "What Is the Purpose of Life?" and begins with the old catechism answer that God made us "to be happy with him forever in the next [world]." That happy togetherness is precisely a relation, the beatific vision.

Then Fr. M notes that "concern for justice is a constitutive element of our faith"—true, but it is hardly the only such element. Hundreds of "constitutive elements" might have been included in this short booklet, but then it wouldn't have been short. It is instructive, I think, that Fr. M notes the lack of a discussion of only one of the cardinal virtues. I wonder why he did not complain that no mention is made of prudence, temperance, and fortitude, especially in view of the fact that the virtue of justice, unless reigned in by the other three, soon ceases to be a virtue at all, as anyone who has had to deal with a person imprudently seeking "justice" will attest.

In summation: This little booklet is a very narrow—and probably, in the end, a very unhealthy presentation of "the Catholic Church and God's plan for you." More and more of this literature floods church vestibules and is passed off on unsuspecting Catholics who are honestly searching for a good compendium of Catholic teaching. I think that the easy availability of this kind of stuff is a good sign that all of us need to become more honestly and faithfully conversant about what being a Catholic at the end of the twentieth century really demands. Just because something says "Catholic" on it does not mean that "Catholic" is in it.

Is *Pillar of Fire, Pillar of Truth* "narrow"? Admittedly it's limited in scope, and, given its purpose—a short introduction to Catholicism for those confused by non-Catholics' questions—the "narrowness" is proper. Would a short introduction to mathematics for the uninitiated include chapters on differential equations, calculus, and the theory of groups?

What about Fr. M's laudable concern for the mental and spiritual health of his parishioners? Is the booklet carrying a contagion that may hurt them? What else can be meant by the term "unhealthy"? I can't avoid concluding that this is a catch-word, what the late social philosopher Richard Weaver termed a "devil term." Such words have no intrinsic meaning. Like expletives heard on street corners, they convey nothing other than a general dislike. I have always thought that traditional four-letter words are actually refuges for people without the intelligence to insult others cleverly. The term "unhealthy," when used in the way the priest uses it, carries some of the same tone and, unfortunately, a bit of the same baggage.

Then Fr. M says something I desperately wish were true: "More and more of this literature floods church vestibules." If church racks were filled with booklets like *Pillar of Fire, Pillar of Truth*, the laity would be far better informed about their faith—something greatly to be prayed and worked for. The solution he proposes to the "flood" he finds so dangerous (and that I, having visited hundreds of vestibules, find so non-existent) is for Catholics "to become more honestly and faithfully conversant about what being a Catholic at the end of the twentieth century really demands." But how can they be "conversant" if they don't know the rudiments of their faith? How can they converse about something they hardly know and attend to largely out of habit? You become conversant about a sport by studying up about it and, perhaps, by participating in it actively. You don't become conversant through an eighth sacrament, holy osmosis.

If Fr. M is saying, under all his words of complaint, that he wants the folks in the pews to go out and engage in social justice work, well, that's fine, even virtuous, but how can we expect them to be so motivated if they can't answer intelligently the opening question of the child's catechism: "Why did God make you?" If they don't understand why God made them, it's unlikely they will see Christ in their neighbors, and, if they don't know why Christ died for them, they won't know why they might need to offer themselves up as holocausts for the people next door.

4

Thumbs Up, Thumbs Down

In conjunction with John Paul II's visits to America in 1993 and 1999, Catholic Answers, the apologetics apostolate I founded and direct, distributed free copies of its most popular booklet, *Pillar of Fire, Pillar of Truth*, to those attending the papal functions in Denver and St. Louis. Staff members and volunteers placed themselves at strategic street corner locations and ended up giving out a third of a million booklets. To cover the costs of these projects, Catholic Answers turned to direct-mail appeals.

We would have liked the booklet printers to donate their materials and labor and for the hotels we stayed in and the airlines we traveled on to give us gratis lodging and transportation, but we were too realistic to expect such largesse. If we were to undertake massive distributions of the booklet, we had to raise funds in advance. As appeal packages go, ours were simple: outer envelope, appeal letter, reply card, reply envelope. Some of the mailings also included a reproduction of the cover of *Pillar of Fire, Pillar of Truth*.

The outer envelope was plainly printed, black ink on white paper, and contained a teaser. The one for the 1993 campaign was "An unpleasant surprise for the Pope in Denver." Teasers are used to induce the recipient to open the envelope. If the envelope isn't opened, the material inside goes to waste. We chose phrases we thought would be intriguing without being sensationalistic. For Denver, we wanted people to wonder which direction the unpleasant surprise might be coming from. Alas, a few people thought the teaser was too emotional. One (see below) even thought it would increase the chances that the Pope would be assaulted.

In the letter I explained that anti-Catholic organizations intended to target Catholics, especially youth, who planned to see the Pope and that Catholic Answers proposed to counter this proselytizing by distributing free copies of *Pillar of Fire, Pillar of Truth* to everyone attending the events. I pointed out that, although many of the people who planned to go were devout, devotion can't be equated with knowledge. Many devout Catholics know their faith poorly and are easy targets for proselytizers.

Altogether we mailed 900,000 packages for the Denver visit, a lesser number for the one in St. Louis. Naturally, we do not have so many names on our house list. We rented test lists from several dozen Catholic publications and organizations. Most of the test lists were of 5,000 names, but a few were larger. We sent letters to those lists and waited for responses. After a few weeks we were able to see which lists pulled well and which pulled poorly. We then "rolled out" the good lists, mailing to all or part of the remainder of the names.

A response as low as one percent is considered good in direct-mail work. If you are prospecting—that is, looking for new names to add to your house list of donors—you might be happy with a response only half that size. At that rate you lose money on the mailing itself, but you end up with the names of people who like what you're doing. If they give to you once, it's likely they will give again. What they give in the future will offset the loss you take now.

We were fortunate in that nearly all of the lists we mailed to made a profit. Our response rate from rented lists averaged one-and-a-half percent, and from our house list we obtained a much higher response rate, as one would expect. Donations varied from a single dollar to more than a thousand dollars. When added together they not only paid for the solicitation campaigns but for the cost of the booklet's printing and distribution.

Although there are about 62 million Catholics in the U.S., the universe of orthodox Catholic names is small, less than two million. This isn't to say the other 60 million Catholics are unorthodox. It just means their names are not on readily-available lists. Each name rented comes from lists of donors to other organizations. The most likely donor to our work is someone who has donated to another group's work. Most donate to more than one organization. If a compiled list of all Catholics in the country were available (no such list exists), we would lose money mailing to a cross-section of the list because the large majority of people on it would not be donors. Our likely response rate would be infinitesimal, far below the break-even point.

When we rent mailing lists from other groups, we try to receive the lists on magnetic tape rather than on printed labels. If we receive them on tape, we can load the names into our computers, compare one list to another, and eliminate most duplicates. Although we mailed out 900,000 packages for our Denver project, we actually rented an additional 200,000 names. By purging the duplicates we saved not only tens of thousands of dollars in printing and postage costs but paper, time, and our readers' aggravation. After all, no one likes to receive a stack of duplicate mailings.

(Brief aside: Our staffers used to be able to tell when a particular Catholic book publisher began its new catalogue mailing. We each would receive multiple copies of the catalogue at our homes —sometimes as many as five or six copies on a single day. One year I received more than twenty copies in the space of a week, testimony that my name appeared on many lists. Apparently the publisher amalgamated numerous lists but didn't check for duplicate names. In recent years we have been getting only one or two catalogues per cycle; the publisher now checks for duplicates.)

Catholic Answers has sophisticated computer programs that help us catch duplicates, but the sophistication goes only so far. The programs can catch exact duplicates—where names and addresses are precisely the same—and near duplicates—where names might be spelled slightly differently (such as "Will Jones" vs. "William Jones") or where street addresses are punctuated differently—but they can't catch larger variations in spelling or addressing. This is why some people received multiple copies of our solicitations.

There is another reason. I mentioned that we prefer to receive mailing lists on magnetic tape. Not all organizations provide names that way. Some provide only printed labels. This causes a double problem. First, we can't compare a printed label, which is not in our computers, to lists of names that are in our computers. (To check thousands of names manually would take so much time as not to be worthwhile.) Second, many of the printed lists contain duplicates within themselves. After all, an organization unable to afford a magnetic tape drive perhaps can't afford a program to eliminate duplicates on its house list. This means that a few people received multiple copies of our letter. It couldn't be helped.

Anytime an organization mails out hundreds of thousands of items, it must expect not only a large number of donations but a large number of notes and letters, most kind, some cranky. Let me share comments scrawled to us on the reply cards or typed as full-blown letters. These may seem amusing, annoying, or touching. I quote more negative than positive comments—not because they were more common (they weren't), but on the principle enunciated by Leo Tolstoy in the opening of *Anna Karenina*: "Happy families are all alike; every unhappy family is unhappy in its own way." There is greater variety among the few negatives than among the many positives, and sometimes we can learn more from the thinking of sourpusses than from the praise of friends.

The most uncomplimentary people exhibited the courage of their anonymity: "Go suck an egg!" "Lousy scum. Poor try!" "You people are nuts!"

Some nameless complainers were longwinded:

> I must inform you that while I understand your good intentions, you are attempting to wage a war on the demons of Protestantism from a very unstable foundation. Your religion is not the Catholic religion; it is the Conciliarist Church that was founded by the bishops of Vatican II and Pope Paul VI. The Holy Roman Catholic religion continues to live and thrive through the Society of St. Pius X. You must understand that Vatican II has turned a once-mighty Church into a pathetic, feel-good, sympathize-with-me Protestant manifestation.

Most people left their names or at least their titles. Let's start with priests. "I do not like the Pope or his policies—I will not support them" (Pastor, Sacred Heart of Jesus Church, Shreveport, Louisiana). In fairness I should note that we mailed our solicitations to 15,000 Catholic pastors; each letter was addressed to "Pastor." We can't tell who at the rectory at this church actually returned the reply card. It could have been a priest other than the pastor, or it could have been the secretary. In any case, the sentiment suggests a problem at one Shreveport parish.

"Not interested in your mailings. Save paper and landfills" (Pastor, St. Stephen's Church, Milwaukee, Wisconsin).

"You should be prosecuted. Do not send this crap again" (Pastor, St. Anthony's Church, Burlington, Vermont).

Some priests with negative comments signed their names:

> On the back cover of the booklet *Pillar of Fire, Pillar of Truth*, there are two statements to which I have disagreements. The first is the sentence, "Jesus established the Catholic Church especially for you." In my seminary study I learned that Jesus did not "establish" any church, but that he very much wanted the Jewish people to develop a new revealed relationship with God. The Catholic Church "evolved" out of the experience of the early Christians. The second statement is, "This is why the Bible calls the Catholic Church the 'pillar and foundation of truth.'" Where does it say that? [Fr. Dan Gardner, Topeka, Kansas]

It says that in 1 Timothy 3:15. I wrote to Fr. Gardner directly, saying that, "If you learned from your seminary studies that Jesus established no church, all I can say is that your instructors did you a disservice. . . . Such a view is incompatible with both pre-Vatican II and post-Vatican II ecclesiology—at least with the ecclesiology taught by the magisterium."

Fr. Gardner's letter echoes one from Maurice Hamington, an assistant professor at Mount St. Mary's College in Los Angeles.

> I was aghast at the lack of biblical and theological background in the literature I received from your organization. For example, the notion that Jesus established a church or that he had a plan for individual Catholics disregards even Catholic biblical scholarship. Your organization smacks of Catholic Fundamentalism, and it does a disservice to the public, particularly those not familiar with bib-

lical, historical criticism. Read such Catholic scholars as Raymond Brown, Joseph Fitzmeyer, and Roland Murphy. Otherwise you are burying your heads in the sand by ignoring what we know about the Bible.

In writing to Prof. Hamington I noted that

most scholars internationally (and historically) readily affirm that Jesus indeed founded a Church and that there is a divine purpose to our existence. Come to think of it, I don't recall any biblical scholar arguing against divine purpose being manifest in Scripture. Yes, we are familiar with the writings of Raymond Brown, Roland Murphy, and Joseph Fitzmyer (whose name you incorrectly spell as Fitzmeyer, which makes me wonder how well you know his works), and we profit from them. We also are familiar with the writings of biblical scholars, both here and abroad, who find occasional fault in the opinions of these men. (We do not hold that certain biblical scholars, such as those you list, are infallible.) We seem to take a more catholic (universal, wide-ranging) approach than you. Do you, for instance, have any familiarity with Evangelical biblical scholars, many of whom surpass their Catholic counterparts in knowledge? Most Catholic Bible scholars seem to be oblivious to the work of Evangelical scholars.

The advance of modern biblical scholarship and of scholarship in allied fields is undercutting the "assured results" [certain] people trumpet. We see this, for example, in such areas as the dating of the books of the New Testament. At first modern scholarship seemed to require later and later datings, but then increased information necessitated earlier and earlier datings. The monopoly position on late datings is crumbling at the edges as honest scholars rethink things from square one, and the monopoly soon may crumble altogether. Ditto with Markan priority. Naturally, those who have built their reputations on such things will hesitate to conceive that their scholarly lives might have taken a wrong turn—amazing, isn't it, what blinders pride can erect?—but I venture to say that it is likely that in half a century the landscape will look quite different and that the Big Names in today's biblical scholarship may no longer be read or remembered.

Most comments we received were from neither priests nor professors, but from regular laymen:

"You are a bunch of fakes!" (Sarah McQuade, Scottsdale, Arizona).

"You should be deeply ashamed for sending out your recent mailing. I have never received such an anti-Christian message. It is an embarrassment to think that you and your organization are soliciting money to pit Christian against Christian" (Karl A. Hakkarainen, Holden, Massachusetts). That's one way to look at it. Another is that we were soliciting money so Catholics, who were going to be confronted by anti-Catholic proselytizers anyway, would have a better chance of keeping and explaining their faith.

"I find your counter-plan as offensive as the purported opposition. Hopefully the Holy Spirit will use the current Bishop of Rome as s/he [sic] did the first one to inspire a renewal—but not along the Fundamentalist lines you propose" (David D. Oakland, Ames, Iowa).

"The jerk in the dress should stay in Rome" (James F. Byrnes, Newark, Ohio).

"I don't want to belong to a church as full of hate for other Christians as you paint the Catholic Church. Thank God you don't speak for all" (Patricia Dahl, Averill, New York). She identified herself as "author, writer, contributor to *Priest* magazine."

"This sounds like a con game. I am reporting it to the Chamber of Commerce and the Diocese of San Diego" (Mrs. V. Flynn, Ormond Beach, Florida). Too late. The Diocese was aware of our plans.

"I am anti-Catholic. Please take my name off your mailing list!" (Marilyn Piland, Springfield, Illinois).

"We believe that attitudes such as yours are unchristian, even uncatholic. Catholic means universal and ecumenical. They only serve to fire up old hates, which is not the work of God, obviously. By the way, we are Catholics, but certainly not your kind" (Simon B. Miranda, Miami, Florida). Mr. Miranda describes himself as "a Catholic Fundamentalist." Go figure.

"You could be the anti-Christ for all we know" (Edward Corcora, Joppa, Maryland).

"Don't send me this stuff again. Our Lord and his Mom are in control in regard to the Pope" (Mike Forgas, Beaumont, Texas).

As a professional fund-raiser, I am insulted by your scare tactics. You have failed to offer any proof that Catholics have been "stolen in the past"—you just base your appeal on the fear that it might happen. Furthermore, you're better off not to put amounts above $1,000 on a reply card, but to go after them by personal solicitation [Karen Brandrick, Seattle, Washington].

The proof you want, Miss Brandrick, is down the street, at Calvary Chapel or the nearest independent Baptist church. Take a head count. As many as half the people will be former Catholics. As far as listing large amounts on the reply card goes, your theory doesn't square with our facts. Several individuals donated more than $1,000, and most of them were people previously unknown to us, just as, we suppose, Catholic Answers was previously unknown to them. Since we otherwise didn't know them, we hardly could have arranged for face-to-face solicitations.

"Why don't you ask for money for birth control? In South America this is needed as they breed like flies. If they would not breed so much, they wouldn't come to America. Hail Mary—you need birth control" (Henry Ziegler, Maynard, Iowa). It's all a plot, Mr. Ziegler. Catholics plan to take over the world by out-populating the opposition. (Isn't demography wonderful?)

"I happen to be one of your so-called separated brethren. You must be aware of the problem your Church has with child abuse. When will your leaders admit the reason for this? What is the reason for not allowing priests and nuns to live a natural life? Get with it!" (Bertil Bengtsson, Deerfield, Illinois). If celibacy caused child abuse, then we'd expect to find a higher percentage of abusers among single adults than among married adults, but we don't. Besides, the psychological factors that lead to child abuse are formed a decade or more before a person is eligible to become a priest or nun. Therefore the religious life itself can't be a cause of the problem.

"I am embarrassed to receive such tasteless, garish, gaudy envelopes. It makes you look like some ignorant, Bible-thumping

group of backwoods hayseeds" (Bill Berg, Saugus, Massachusetts).
The outer envelope was printed in black ink on white stock. This
is "garish, gaudy"?

> I must inform you that I shall not send you one red penny. It is
> my firmly held belief that it is about time that this pope was "un-
> pleasantly surprised," and not just by the activities of the Funda-
> mentalists. Most dioceses haven't taught Catholicism in decades. If
> John Paul II wants to continue traipsing around the world with his
> head in the sand [an odd image—think about it], that is his choice,
> but I do not have to be a party to it [James G. Davis, Fayetteville,
> North Carolina].

Some folks have a tendency to blow things out of proportion.
"I am grossly offended by your use of a mailing envelope indiscriminately scrawled with incendiary phraseology ["An unpleasant
surprise for the Pope in Denver. . ."]. This irresponsible effort
to gain attention for your publication could further endanger the
Holy Father" (Margaret Brick, Hemet, California). Come again?
"I wrote the Pope a few years ago and told him my Church
was destroyed [by not providing the old Latin Mass]. He never
answered me" (Mary Skrha, Cleveland, Ohio). Have a heart, Mrs.
Skrha. If I have trouble answering the relatively few letters I receive, understand that the Pope has no time to answer the zillions
of letters he receives.

> Did you ever wonder why there are so many ex-Catholics fighting
> the Church? Maybe they are disillusioned by the sexist male bu-
> reaucracy that is only interested in perpetuating itself. I hope the
> Pope listens instead of speaking and making a fool of himself. If
> you like, join us in praying for a woman pope [Arthur D. Moore,
> Bloomfield Hills, Michigan].

Those ex-Catholics who leave the Church and fight it are almost exclusively conservative Christians now. Male bureaucra-
cies didn't bother them before and don't bother them now. Those
who decry "sexism," who worry about their not having a big
enough share of power in the Church (and power is what they're
really after, of course), and who stump for women priests—these

folks rarely leave the Church. They don't seem to have the courage
of their convictions.

Some letters we received are not printable in their entirety. One
was from James Van Slyke of New York City:

> You are an a—h—. You equate religious faith with money. I re-
> peat, you're an a—h—. In your appeal you state, "We pray that
> you will be one of these donors." If this "prayer" is true, it is not
> directed to Christ. It is directed to money. I repeat, you're an a—
> h—.

The format of his comment leads me to suspect that Mr. Van
Slyke served in the Army and there imbibed the tripartite rule of
military instruction: Tell them what you're going to tell them,
then tell them, then tell them what you've told them.

Happily, most critical comments were couched in repeatable
words:

> In my opinion the Church is a failure because timid priests and
> bishops have allowed popular social and political beliefs to usurp the
> foundations of the Church. One can no longer trust the Church. If
> I give money to any religious group, you may be assured it will not
> be to any Catholic organization. I honestly believe most priests and
> bishops will do well to save themselves, and I am willing to face
> judgment without their help. People have lost a lot as the Catholic
> Church self-destructed, protecting the misfits within its ranks and
> refusing to stand for what is right [James C. Thornton, Canon
> City, Colorado].

> I disagree with you in your attempt to hide the truth from young
> Catholics. I feel it is time we stop playing around with the false
> teachings of our Church and tell our people the truth for once. If
> we lose members, then we will be the better for it. The Catholic
> Church was not established by Jesus; in fact, he never built a church.
> It was the disciplines [sic] who began the Church by holding home
> meetings. They were not what we could call a Catholic Church,
> and by no means was there such as thing as a pope in their church.
> I am no longer a Catholic—I have found Jesus [Milton L. Pack,
> Bryan, Texas].

I am a product of sixteen years of Catholic education. Yet it took forty-five years before the Lord showed me the way to salvation was through Jesus Christ. Hopefully this shield you are putting around the [people who will see the Pope] will not be strong enough to keep out the truth. I am not anti-Catholic or Protestant; I am a saved Christian [Pete Bogan, Morristown, New Jersey].

Please take me off your mailing list! Your letter sounds to me like a bunch of crazies trying to frighten the public about those big, bad Fundamentalists. Give me a break! As a child, I can remember a group that gathered on the street corner on Sunday evening and preached fire and brimstone. They were from the Pillar of Fire Church! They were laughable, and your group sounds like it's following close behind! Was "prosylatize" [sic] a new word you learned this year? [Elizabeth Kash, Brooklyn, New York].

"I am one of those former Catholics you talk about. I regret all the years I spent in a dead religion, so please don't ask me to contribute to a church that kept me from knowing the Lord" (Elaine D. Landry, Estherwood, Louisiana).

"I can't locate you or your organization in my Catholic directory. Please remove me from your mailing list" (George Barclay, Riverdale, Georgia). Catholic Answers is listed in *The Official Catholic Directory*, under the Diocese of San Diego—not as an arm of the Diocese (Catholic Answers is an independent lay-run group) but as an approved organization.

Sometimes you run into a case of mistaken identity.

I've given hundreds of dollars to the Keatings for anti-porn and good causes, and I and many others have been betrayed. You know the story. I saved my meager earnings to give to Charles Keating, and I'm not being suckered again!" [Eleanor M. Sprossler, West Orange, New Jersey].

True story: A few years ago I was to speak at the Mission San Diego de Alcalá, founded by Blessed Junipero Serra in 1769. The then-pastor was a long-time acquaintance of mine. Perhaps recent newspaper headlines were on his mind as he introduced me as "Charles Keating." As soon as he stepped away from the microphone he realized what he had done. "Not to worry," I whispered. I greeted the audience and said,

> I assure you that I am not now, nor have I ever been, affiliated with Lincoln Savings and Loan, and my first name is 'Karl,' not 'Charles,' and I am no relation to the former financier—but I wish I had known him when he was passing out the cash.

The audience had a good laugh.

Some people have confused ideas of their ecclesiastical rights:

> I received the letter pleading for money, so I decided to reply. I was a Catholic since 1945, but now I claim to be a born-again Christian. The Catholic Church did not lead me to the Lord. I cannot believe that the Catholic Church is the one, true church. I am refused Holy Communion in the Catholic Church. I wonder, "What does my friend Jesus think about that?" [L. Kingsley, Hudson, Michigan].

Mrs. Kingsley, the best I can do is to tell you what I think about your not being permitted to receive Communion: I think it makes good sense. You no longer are a Catholic. You do not believe the Catholic Church is Jesus' Church. You have no unity of faith with Catholics. Why, then, should you be allowed to receive Communion, the great sign of unity of faith? Wouldn't you be proclaiming through your action what you do not believe in your mind?

> You say you are going to send me a free copy [of *Pillar of Fire, Pillar of Truth*] after I mail you a donation. Who's fooling who? How can this book be free if you want a donation for it? This is the first time you wrote to me, and you don't even have the decency to give me the name of the person or place that had the nerve to give my name and address to you without my permission [Linda Della-Badia, Brooklyn, New York].

The booklet was given out free to the people who attended the papal events, Mrs. Della-Badia. We received your name from a charitable foundation that schools American Indian children and that rents its mailing list to other organizations.

> I don't share your belief that Fundamentalists are the root of all evil. I think the Catholic Church has to restudy its teachings. I do not

believe that the Catholic Church is the only true church and that all other churches are false. Don't get me wrong. I am in no way putting down the Pope. He is a very gracious and peaceful man, and I am sure he shares my beliefs [Susan Cochran, Wilmington Delaware].

Miss Cochran describes herself as "a Catholic youth." She will need to amend that to "a disappointed Catholic youth" once she discovers the Pope doesn't share her belief that the Catholic Church is not the only true church. Yes, he acknowledges that other churches contain elements of truth, so it is proper to say their tenets are partly true. But if they are only partly true, they must be partly false also. Miss Cochran seems to be a prime example of the well-intentioned but inadequately-formed young Catholic. After all, a Catholic who protests that there really isn't much difference between Catholicism and other religions—at least not any difference that should be determining—is precisely the kind of Catholic who, presented with a few beguilingly solid arguments, is likely to "unpope."

Brunella McLaren of Runge, Texas wrote that her local priest assured her Catholic Answers was crying wolf. "He said that the young Catholics will not come in contact with these non-Catholic people, as they will be cordoned off and away from activities. These kids will probably toss [*Pillar of Fire, Pillar of Truth*] in their suitcases, if you're lucky, and never look at them again." Wrong on two counts, Mrs. McLaren. The anti-Catholic Fundamentalists were not cordoned off from the Catholic participants. They were stationed, dozens of them, on the street corners immediately surrounding venues at which the Pope was to speak. You couldn't walk a block without walking past several proselytizers. Some even stood on median strips, accosting everyone using the crosswalks. As for the recipients' attitude toward *Pillar of Fire, Pillar of Truth*, the booklet seemed to be the most sought-after piece of literature in town—sought after and kept. By the end of the event, whenever our volunteers asked people if they had received copies, in unison they'd reach into their knapsacks or back pockets, pull out a copy, and grin.

Perhaps the most interesting note came from Feliz A. Sczubelek of Newark, Delaware. Apparently he is on everyone's list and doesn't like it one bit. He sent a form letter detailing the number of solicitations received over the course of a year. "Last year, for example, I received 527 letters requesting donations, 169 from various Catholic charities and missions." These included 31 solicitations from Indian schools, 14 from law enforcement groups, 28 from senior citizen groups, and 78 from health insurance providers. He also received 15 calendars.

Some people thought our solicitation didn't give Catholics enough credit. "Have you so little confidence in our people?" asked Barbara Narayan of Lubbock, Texas.

> I have been teaching Catholic religion classes for some twenty-five years, and I certainly believe that the majority of those I have taught know why they are Catholic and could discuss this with anyone, even the "dangerous" Fundamentalists you mention. If this is not the case, I daresay we are doing a lousy job of educating. Including our people in parish activities and ministries will go a lot farther toward keeping them in the Church than some pamphlet.

Mrs. Narayan must be a fine teacher, if the majority of her students can hold their own with Fundamentalists; she must give her students a solid grounding in the doctrines of the faith. Our experience has shown such success to be rare. Most education programs ill equip parishioners to explain or defend their faith. The simple fact is that, yes, "we are doing a lousy job of educating." But, no, including folks "in parish activities and ministries" is not, as such, the answer. Such inclusion does nothing for their minds; besides, they can be as "ministerially active" at Good Book Baptist as at their present parishes.

If Catholics are susceptible to Fundamentalist blandishments, maybe we should engage in a little benign neglect. That is the opinion a few people expressed, including Fr. Rian Clancy, a Passionist priest from Chicago.

> Your appalling appeal just crossed my unbelieving eyes. First it was Communism, and now it's Fundamentalism. If these innocents are to be seduced at a papal visit, they mustn't have much in the way

of faith. Leave these people alone and let go and let God. If their
faith/religion is that fragile, they better not go to Rome.

The opening words of Fr. Clancy's letter remind me of an anec-
dote set in the 1956 presidential election. Adlai Stevenson, the
Democratic candidate, attended a religious service at which Norman Vincent Peale preached. The sermon was based on one of
the Pauline letters. As he descended the church steps, Stevenson
was asked by reporters what he thought of the service. He said,
"I find Paul appealing and Peale appalling."

Here is something else Stevenson may have found appalling.
Ron Webster, of Colville, Washington, proffered what he considered to be a sure-fire technique for dealing with vocal anti-
Catholics: "Tell 'em you love 'em, share a donut and a cup of
coffee, give 'em all a hug, a nice hug."

One mother, whose name I will withhold, wrote,

> I share your concern, not just for the young people who are going
> to see the Pope, but for all Catholic teens and young adults. I have
> a teenage son who, although confirmed, doesn't give much time
> or thought to religion or the Church. I've taken time to talk to
> him about people who would try to convert him away from his
> Catholic faith, but I know he finds it hard to believe that it could
> be a friend or relative or someone his own age.

This woman spent several years away from the Church, "at first
allured by secular and humanist ideas and later because of misconceptions promoted by 'born-again' Fundamentalist friends. I
know the value of the pamphlets you are printing."

She understands the vectors in society. So does Juliana Mc-
Caskill of Redwood City, California, who says, "I converted to
the Catholic faith four years ago, and I have never seen a group
of people with such little knowledge of their own religion. It
makes me very sad to have to defend my faith to people that are
supposed to be in my own religion." When Mrs. McCaskill had
questions about the Bible, she approached the rector at her local
seminary. "I was very disappointed in him. He could not answer
any question I had but only suggested that I purchase the *Jerome
Biblical Commentary*. When I finally did convert, I visited him and

told him about *Catholicism and Fundamentalism*. I told him that he needed to read it and let his students read it." (Thanks for the endorsement, Mrs. McCaskill.)

Some letters were long, others short. The shortest was from Rev. Richard C. Mushorn, the vicar of St. Mark the Evangelist Episcopal Church in North Bellmore, New York: "Good job!" Perhaps the most touching was from Kristina MacLaren of Colorado Springs, Colorado: "I am only 12, but I assure you that I have sent as much as possible. I am glad that you are out there to support the youth of my faith." Equally kind was a note from Fr. Joseph M. Sherer, a Dominican living at St. Dominic's Priory in Washington, D.C.: "Many thanks for the wonderful work you are doing in defense of the Church. I am half blind and 92, retired. Enclosed please find another $20."

A woman from St. Charles, Missouri, boosted our spirits with this note: "I will not be there. My husband is partly blind and has a bad knee. So we stay home. I will be praying for all of you. Sorry I did not send some help sooner. We live on a limited income." Another woman, resident at the Fort Bayard Medical Center in Fort Bayard, New Mexico, explained that she couldn't help financially—"I am 83 years old; my savings, Social Security, and retirement pay are going to pay medical board and room"—but she promised to "pass the word" about our project.

Fr. M. V. Iorio, of Acra, New York, wrote, "We cannot help you financially, but we (my prayer warriors and I) will be praying for you and your great work, especially during the Holy Father's visit." He was joined in intention by a woman in Chicago, who described herself as "an old woman living on SSI and unable to work outside the home. I am poor. I will pray for the success of your endeavor."

From Woodland Hills, California, came a note from Fr. Alden Sison, who said,

> The proof sheet cover looks great. Even more so, the little blurb will surely attract Catholics and non-Catholics alike. It unashamedly proclaims the truth: The Catholic Church is the Church Christ founded. Let's give these Fundamentalists a run for their money.

Rosalie Pezon, of Haines City, Florida, said that "a charitable soul in my prayer group passed around the wonderful plan you have to reach people at the Pope's visit. The printer's proof sheet is excellent. I am so happy to help financially. Hope we reach them all with our prayers and action." We did not reach every participant, but we came close. Our staff and volunteers had trouble finding Catholics who did not have a copy of *Pillar of Fire, Pillar of Truth*.

Of all the replies to our solicitation, our favorite (posted on the bulletin board in the staff kitchen) was from "The Smith Family," city unknown:

> This family is anti-Catholic, so please stop sending us your lies and propaganda! Go sprinkle some water on your forehead, go tell your wrong-doings to a common man (don't go directly to God by praying for forgiveness), and keep praying to your man-made saints, but leave us alone and please take us off any mailing lists the Catholics have us on. Also, don't send us any of these statues, beads, water, or other trinkets. We don't need you to pray for us on a pagan day (Sunday). We prefer to obey the commandment of worshiping on the Sabbath day.

Whew!

5

Evolving the Pope's Words

On dark Mediterranean nights the ancients observed the movements of the planets and stars, and during the day they observed the movement of the sun. They noticed general regularity marked by particular irregularity. Movements shifted slowly during the year, the sun rising and setting farther to the north, then farther to the south, the planets swimming among the stars, racing one another through the constellations, sometimes overtaking one another, sometimes apparently moving backward. Even the stars themselves processed through the skies.

Since man is incapable of *not* drawing inferences from observations, the ancients guessed at the arrangement of heavenly bodies. Some surmised that the sun, like a candle quenched in a bowl, was extinguished each evening as it was swallowed by the sea. Others thought this improbable and speculated that the sun circled behind the earth at night. Even to the unsophisticated, the planets and stars seemed ordered; perhaps they too circled the earth. Thus there arose astronomical hypotheses.

Proto-astronomers, such as the Wise Men of Matthew's Gospel, went further, carefully measuring the movements, keeping records of the rising and setting of the sun, the journeys of the planets, the positions of the stars. The accuracy of their measurements was limited by the power of the naked eye and the absence of chronometers, yet they adduced evidence, applied it to the prevailing hypotheses, and ended up with theories, which are hypotheses united with evidence that tends to support them. The longest-lasting and most influential was that of Ptolemy, who, relying on earlier observers such as Hipparchus and Timocharis, developed a geocentric theory that seemed to account for all observed movements—as the medievals later put it, his theory "saved the appearances." For centuries few doubted that the earth stood at the center of what today we call the solar system.

But the Ptolemaic theory, raised from mere hypothesis through the application of scientific measurements, proved in the end to be false. The sun, not the earth, is the center of the solar system; the planets move along ellipses, not along cycles and epicycles; the stars, so distant that their movements are almost imperceptible, do not circle the earth, but are, for practical purposes, fixed.

Thus it is in science. Initial observation produces hypotheses, which are mere guesses, some immediately seen to be improbable (such as that the setting sun is extinguished each day), some seen to be possible (such as that the sun, planets, and stars circle the earth). Through scientific investigation and the gathering of innumerable tiny facts, scientists come to single out one hypothesis and produce an overarching explanation that accommodates the evidence. This explanation is called a theory.

But a theory is not the same as a truth. A theory may be true, or it may be false. Aristotelian physics was supplanted by Newtonian physics, which in turn was supplanted by Einsteinian physics, which, in all likelihood, will be supplanted by something else. Newton thought there to be no necessary limit to the speed of light in a vacuum. Einstein demonstrated that the speed of light is a constant. Today some scientists speculate that Einstein erred and that Newton may have been right after all.

This brings us to the theory of evolution and to Pope John Paul II's statement to the Pontifical Academy of Sciences. It is not my purpose to comment on evolution per se; I do not propose to address its merits or demerits. I just want to look at what the Pope said and how a prominent evolutionist, Stephen Jay Gould, understood (or misunderstood) the papal statement.

Gould is professor of biology, geology, and the history of science at Harvard and is perhaps the best-known popularizer of evolution. He calls himself a Jewish agnostic: "I am not, personally, a believer or a religious man in any sense of institutional commitment or practice. But I have enormous respect for religion, and the subject has always fascinated me, beyond almost all others (with a few exceptions, like evolution, paleontology, and baseball)." In a lengthy and well-crafted essay in *Natural History* magazine, he argued that religion and science are separate domains, each with its own magisterium. There is no necessary conflict between the two. Gould sees science as covering "the empirical universe: what is it made of (fact) and why does it work this way (theory)." Religion, by contrast, "extends over questions of moral meaning and value."

Of course, this is not a differentiation that a Christian will be satisfied with. Although every revealed dogma has something to do with "questions of moral meaning and value," the faith can't be straitjacketed. It also deals with "physical" facts: the Son taking flesh and living on earth at a particular time and in a particular place, the return from the dead of his material (not imaginary) body, the establishment of a Church which, while having an invisible spiritual dimension, is composed of physical human beings. All these things are subject to scientific investigation, as are all historical events.

Was Abraham Lincoln a real person or a fictional character? No one living today could have had a chance to see him and to judge directly, but his existence, like the existence of an antediluvian stegosaurus or of a modern lily, is subject to scientific investigation, to proof that relies on the application of the five senses and on inferences drawn from measurements. When I was a boy, there still lived veterans of the Civil War. It is possible that one of those survivors had met Lincoln. If so, then there was a living witness to Lincoln's existence, and the testimony of that witness would have been subject to scientific investigation.

Then there are the daguerreotypes of Matthew Brady, those haunting images in which we see Lincoln (or at least what purports to be Lincoln) in profile, rigidly looking at something outside the camera's range. Are the photographs authentic or faked? That is something for scientific investigation to determine.

We also have books and other documents about Lincoln. They

are filled with testimonies of people who knew and worked with him, of people who knew and opposed him. These are evidentiary exhibits, each subject to scientific investigation, the way fossils are subject to investigation.

Gould, for all his scientific learning and literary art, fails to delineate properly the spheres of science and religion. There is an overlap, and it won't do to restrict religion to "questions of moral meaning and value," as though those questions have no interplay with the material world. That said, let me turn, finally, to the central part of Gould's long essay, the whole of which occupies six pages of text. Gould is concerned with comparing John Paul II's statement to *Humani Generis*, an encyclical by Pius XII. He wants to see if the Catholic Church has made "progress" in its understanding of evolution, and he concludes it has.

Gould notes that

> Pius writes the well-known words that permit Catholics to entertain the evolution of the human body . . . so long as they accept the divine creation and infusion of the soul. . . . In short, Pius forcefully proclaimed that, while evolution may be legitimate in principle, the theory, in fact, had not been proven and might be entirely wrong. One gets the strong impression, moreover, that Pius was rooting pretty hard for a verdict of falsity.

John Paul reiterates his predecessor's teaching that the idea of the evolution of the body is not itself opposed to Catholic doctrine. "The novelty and news value of John Paul's statement," says Gould, "lies, rather, in his profound revision of Pius's second and rarely quoted claim that evolution, while conceivable in principle and reconcilable with religion, can cite little persuasive evidence and may well be false." The present pope, thinks Gould, has taught "that evolution can no longer be doubted by people of good will."

Gould quotes from the Holy Father's October 23, 1996, address to the Pontifical Academy of Sciences:

> Today, almost half a century after the publication of the encyclical [*Humani Generis*], new knowledge has led to the recognition

of more than one hypothesis in the theory of evolution. It is indeed remarkable that this theory has been progressively accepted by researchers, following a series of discoveries in various fields of knowledge. The convergence, neither sought nor fabricated, of the results of work that was conducted independently is in itself a significant argument in favor of the theory.

This is how Gould interprets these lines: "John Paul . . . adds that additional data and theory have placed the factuality of evolution beyond reasonable doubt. Sincere Christians must now accept evolution not merely as a plausible possibility but also as an effectively proven fact." We now have "John Paul's entirely welcoming 'it has been proven true.'"

Suddenly one's admiration for Gould wanes—no longer is he a careful parser of papal statements. He has been transformed into the ideologue, pressing himself to a conclusion that the facts he has served up just don't demonstrate. He seriously misconstrues John Paul's words. For one thing, Gould uses a bogus translation. (I should point out that this was not his fault; early reports of the speech gave an incorrect rendering.) The Holy Father did not say that there is "more than one hypothesis in the theory of evolution." The French original reads *"plus qu'une hypothèse."* The Pope said evolution is "more than a hypothesis." And what is "more" than a hypothesis, which is nothing other than an intelligent guess? The next step up is a theory, which is a hypothesis for which scientific evidence has been adduced. Theories, as followers of Ptolemy learned, may be true or false. They are provisional explanations based on observation and measurement, but they are distinct from incontrovertible truths.

If you search the Pope's statement, you will find nothing that supports Gould's assertion that "additional data and theory have placed the factuality of evolution beyond reasonable doubt." The Pope doesn't use the phrase "beyond reasonable doubt" or anything like it. He doesn't say that evolution has progressed beyond the level of a theory. He says merely that, from multiple disciplines, scientific evidence has been gathered and that the evidence is "a significant argument in favor of the theory"—not a conclusive argument, but a strong argument.

Nowhere does John Paul assert that "sincere Christians must now accept evolution not merely as a plausible possibility but also as an effectively proven fact." He does not claim that the theory "has been proven true." The Pope's reticence to say such things —if he believed them, he could have said them plainly, after all —more rightly should lead a reader to suspect that the Pope is not entirely convinced that evolution is true. The theory is still that—just a theory. It's more than a hypothesis, since there seems to be substantial evidence in its favor, but there was substantial evidence in favor of Ptolemy's theory too.

Reading Gould's essay (which, except at this point, is not tendentious and doesn't attempt to draw more from papal statements than those statements actually hold), one senses a desperation. Gould tries too hard to get John Paul to say what he wants him to say—so hard that he deliberately puts words into the Pope's mouth. (Given the disparity between what the Pope actually said and Gould's sharply contrasting paraphrase of it, I don't think that's too strong a judgment.)

Nowhere in his essay does Gould advert to problems with evolution. Darwinism, which has been the chief explanation of *how* evolution works (through slow, almost imperceptible changes), is in trouble. In recent years learned books have argued that the perfecting of science has shown Darwinism to be untenable. The missing links are still missing. There is no reasonable way that a protracted series of minute changes can turn, say, a sun-sensitive blot on the skin into an eye. Living things are far more complex, especially at the microscopic level, than Darwin could have imagined.

Even unwavering evolutionists such as Gould have admitted that Darwinism is on shaky legs. Many of them have rejected Darwin's notion of small mutations adding up, over millions of years, into a positive alteration that allows the fit to be even more survivable. These evolutionists have proposed an alternative, "punctuated equilibrium." Instead of a long series of minute changes, there is one spectacular mutation: The blot becomes a fully developed eye in a single or perhaps in a handful of generations, not in thousands of generations. This idea has problems of its own and has not received universal acceptance among evolutionists.

Taking all this together—new books that argue that Darwin got it wrong, plus Darwinists' implicit acknowledgement that Darwinism has problems—we can envision this scenario: Darwinism, the chief explanation of how evolution does what it is supposed to do, is seen to be unsalvageable. It must be abandoned, to be replaced by—what? So far there is no alternative, which means that evolutionists might find themselves in an anomalous position: arguing that evolution is true but unable to explain how it might occur. If *that* point is reached, the whole theory might be junked as untenable. I'm not saying that this is likely, but, given the unsettled state of evolution as a theory, it is possible.

So what is the Holy Father's bottom-line position on evolution? He *didn't* say what Gould imagines that he said, which is that evolution is indubitably true. For this Pope evolution remains a theory —a step up from a mere hypothesis, but a step below a truth. He told the Pontifical Academy of Sciences that "a theory's validity depends on whether or not it can be verified" by being "constantly tested against the facts." A theory must be "rethought" if it "no longer can explain" the facts. John Paul knows what a theory is and what it isn't, and he also knows the history of science. He realizes that today's scientific certainty may be tomorrow's also-ran. While praising scientists for trying to "save the appearances," the Pope can't forget what happened to Ptolemy.

6

Going Down in Flames

The National Catholic Reporter carried an article by its editor, Thomas C. Fox, encouraging its readers to sign up with certain Internet lists (online discussion groups). Seeing an avenue by which our readers might promote the faith, we invited them to join the same lists. If nothing else, we figured, they might be able to offer some ideological balance. The members of at least one list, Sister-L (that is, "Sister List"), were not amused. Their list is devoted to the discussion of the religious life from a feminist perspective, and they bombarded me with angry messages—to use online jargon, they "flamed" me.

Below I give some of the messages and my responses to them. Keep in mind that my responses were written on the fly; they were not products of leisure and therefore not as well phrased or as temperate as they might have been had the clock not been running. I offer them not as models to follow, but to show a real-life, unedited commentary.

To: Kenneth [sic] Keating

In your magazine, you included a report on the *NCR* article on Internet lists. It said, among other things:

> *The National Catholic Reporter*, in its October 28 issue, ran an article about Catholics using the Internet. Thomas C. Fox recommended several e-mail lists to the liberal readership of *NCR*. We recommend those same lists, but for a different reason. By signing up you can counter the self-satisfaction of the heterodox for whom these lists are intended. This is a fine way to engage in long-distance apologetics. You need have no worry about receiving unwelcomed

visitors at your door or strange missives in the regular mail. In each case, when you subscribe using your e-mail program, leave the subject line blank. When writing your name, do not include the square brackets. . . . Fox describes [Sister-L] as dealing with the "history and contemporary concerns of women religious," which means the usual concerns of radical feminists. To subscribe, write to *listserv@suvm.syr.edu.* In the message area write *subscribe sister-l [your name]* . . . If you engage in this cyberspace apostolate, please drop us a line and let us know how you fare (kkeating@aol.com). Inquiring minds want to know.

As co-owner of Sister-L, I would like to know on what basis you make the allegation in print that the meaning of our official description means "the usual concerns of radical feminists." Any evidence you have for this potentially libelous charge would be greatly appreciated. For your information, I sent an announcement of the list, when it began, to the CMSWR [Conference of Major Superiors of Women Religious, the leadership group for more conservative religious]. Surely I would not have done this if the purpose of the list was to push a radical feminist agenda (whatever that is!). There are no litmus tests for subscriptions [memberships]. However, the list does have stated purposes, and ideologically-motivated politicizing is not one of them.

Should any of your readers decide to try to transform the list into a forum for your apologetical agenda, I can assure you that it will not be tolerated. The article from which I have quoted does not, it seems to me, represent responsible journalism.

Margaret Susan Thompson, Ph.D.
cc: Sr. Ritamary Bradley
(co-owner, Sister-L)

Dear Prof. Thompson:

Thank you for clearing up a confusion. I had been under the impression that Tom Fox would recommend a women's list only if it adhered to the feminist line. Perhaps I wrote rashly and Sister-L is intended to express the concerns primarily of, say, sisters associated with Mother Teresa and Mother Angelica. I note with satisfaction that you consider it potentially libelous to be accused of founding a list that caters to the concerns of radical feminists. As you know, one can claim that a phrase is potentially libelous if it falsely imputes to another something such as a loathsome disease. (Ah, there's my legal background peeking out!) It's encouraging to know that you consider feminism to be loathsome.

You say that "any evidence you have for this potentially libelous charge would be greatly appreciated." I suppose we both will see the evidence as we download exchanges from the list, won't we? If it turns out that Sister-L is not a vehicle for feminism, we gladly will print a retraction. (We especially look forward to the list's founders' explanation of why the Holy Father was correct in *Ordinatio Sacerdotalis*.)

By the way, we did not suggest that there is a litmus test to subscribe to the list. Had that been our understanding, we would not have recommended that our readers subscribe. After all, most of them would fail the only kind of litmus test we could imagine such a list having.

Thank you for your message. May God continue to keep you in his mercy.

Karl Keating

P.S. My name isn't Kenneth Keating. Perhaps you have me mixed up with the one-time U.S. Senator? Of course, he was around many years ago . . .

To: KKeating

I have asked the postmaster at AOL [America Online] to discuss with you the inappropriateness of the following post: . . ."If you engage in this cyberspace apostolate, please drop us a line and let us know how you fare (kkeating@aol.com). Inquiring minds want to know." I would urge you to print a retraction to those to whom it was sent.

Terri Powell

Miss Powell:

Before you start denouncing people to the authorities, à la Joe McCarthy, please get your facts straight—which you could have done by e-mailing me first. What you think was a post on the Internet was no such thing. It was part of an article in a print magazine. The article mentioned several Internet lists, and someone on one of those lists incorporated part of the text of the article in her own Internet post.

Neither the article nor any of the Internet lists has anything to do with AOL, and AOL was not even mentioned in the article, so I can't see why you think it necessary to bring AOL into the matter. In your quotation you put in parentheses my AOL address, as though I was soliciting an e-mail reply from the readers. But the material in parentheses did not appear in the magazine, and the phrase "drop us a line," as everyone knows, means "send us a letter by U.S. mail."

I hope in the future you will give more consideration to people's free speech rights and will get your facts straight. Do you think I should contact the people who run [your Internet provider] and complain that you have been spreading false information and request that they reprimand you? It seems that you are the one who should circulate a retraction.

Karl Keating

To Mr. Keating:

How shocking to read your article in *This Rock* deriding Sister-L and other lists suggested by *The National Catholic Reporter*. More shocking, further, is your invitation to disturb the dialogue among those for whom the lists were created. I know of nothing in the Gospels, in civilized morality, or in Church orthodoxy that would approve of such tactics. Of course, your proposed plan of action does closely resemble the pre-adolescent mischief of young boys who tramp down others' tomato patches just to cause grief. Perhaps your program is more closely akin to window breaking and laying banana skins in the path of the unwary walker. "The usual concerns of radical feminists"? You have resorted to a smear word, without specified content, but designed to spread ill-will at the very least. What are "radical feminists," and what are their "usual concerns"?

Have you carefully read the introductions sent by many Sister-L subscribers and decided that all these people—scholars, nuns of many decades, wheel-chair bound religious, friends of women religious, inquirers, members of professional societies, etc., deserve your pre-judgment, disdain, and disruption? How dare you imply that you and those you invite to your program are the orthodox and the subscribers to Sister-L are the heterodox? Would you please take your adolescent mischief elsewhere? You have a strangely-twisted notion of apostolate, as well as apparent ignorance of the norms that are to make cyberspace a realm of respectful dialogue and exchange. My dear friend, the age of the Crusades is long past, and the Church does not glory in the violence it occasioned. Again: Please grow up!

> Ritamary Bradley,
> Professor Emerita
> St. Ambrose University,
> Davenport, Iowa

Dear Sr. Bradley:

As you will recall, it was Claude Rains, in *Casablanca*, who had that great line, which went something like this: "I am shocked—shocked I say—to discover there is gambling going on at Rick's." At which point the croupier handed Rains his winnings. It was an amusing scene, and so it is amusing to find that you think it "shocking" for *This Rock* to "deride" (your word) the lists recommended by *The National Catholic Reporter*. And you find it more shocking that we could suggest to our readers that they subscribe to the lists and participate in the exchanges. It was our impression that, when Mr. Fox wrote his invitation, he meant it to apply to all who came across his article. He is a sophisticated man and no doubt knows that not everyone who subscribes to his newspaper agrees with the opinions expressed in it.

You say that you "know of nothing in the Gospels, in civilized morality, or in Church orthodoxy that would approve of such tactics." Don't you sense that you've gone overboard here? Granted, there's nothing in the Gospels about responding to open invitations to subscribe to Internet lists, and perhaps, in the name of civilized morality, this whole matter should be brought up to the U.N. General Assembly or at least to the World Health Organization. But don't you think its stretching matters a bit to wrap these lists in the mantle of Church orthodoxy? After all, they no doubt will be forums to promote such things as women's ordination, the use of contraception, abortion (at least in some circumstances), and idolatry ("goddess spirituality," as Mr. Fox put it). Not a single one of these falls under the rubric of orthodox, unless one feels an irresistible political impulse to adopt even inapplicable terms.

You want to know how I dare to imply that people who support my apostolate are the orthodox while the subscribers to Sister-L are the heterodox. Easy. I use litmus tests. When subscribers to Sister-L can write that they accept without reservation the teaching of *Humanae Vitae*, I happily will confer on them the title orthodox. But for those who reject authoritative teachings of the Church, whether on this or any other matter, they settle upon themselves the apt title heterodox, which, as you know, comes from Greek words meaning "contrary opinion"—in this case, contrary to the Church.

I must say, as I said in my reply to Prof. Thompson's message, that I am pleased to learn that you think it is a smear to accuse someone of being a feminist. This, at least, is encouraging.

Karl Keating

Dear Mr. Keating,

First, my apologies for attributing the wrong first name to you; I hope you will forgive that.

On Sister-L, we do not limit discussion of religious life to any one vision of what that vocation is all about. Some of our subscribers are feminist (though, again, what "radical feminist" is, in your view, is not clear from either the magazine excerpt or your message to me). Some are not feminist. We try not to judge individuals or to attach labels to them. For the record (apparently you are an attorney?), I do think of myself as a feminist.

But, since we have no questionnaire or other litmus test for subscribers, except that they be respectful of the religious vocation and of honest dialogue about it, I have no idea how many others on the list (now about 350) would think of themselves that way. And it doesn't matter! So, no, I do not find feminism "loathsome." What is more, since both the Holy Father and the U.S. bishops have called for recognition of the full equality of women and men, I don't suppose they do, either. The most fundamental meaning of feminism is, of course, recognition of that equality and of the full human potential of women. While I do not have my copy of John Paul's writings in front of me, I do know that he has stated his conviction on this matter clearly and repeatedly.

I'm sure there are many matters on which you and I would differ. For that matter, I know there are many matters on which the various subscribers of Sister-L differ! Still, those who have been on the list have remarked on its supportiveness, its spirit of charity, and its joy. I think we can agree that these are Christian values worth praising wherever they are to be found.

Margaret Susan Thompson

Dear Prof. Thompson:

Thank you for your reply. I'm pleased to learn that Sister-L is a list that encourages honest dialogue among people whose opinions may differ and that it doesn't matter whether subscribers are feminists or not. That will be encouraging news to non-feminists who may wish to participate on a equal basis with feminists. After all, if we agree that there is an equality between men and women, certainly there must be an equality between feminist women and non-feminist women (and between feminist men and non-feminist men).

Yes, you are correct in stating that the Holy Father has given his view repeatedly, though I think you will agree that not many people would describe his view as pro-feminist; a better phrase might be pro-feminine. However that may be, I hope your list will encourage so much diversity of opinion that even Catholics who disagree with feminism will be welcome.

Karl Keating

To: KKeating

I would request that you make a public correction to your stance. The Internet is not a place for this such behavior. One of the major rules of Netiquette [Internet etiquette] is not to get on a list simply to disagree with or convert the people on the list.

Also, from America Online's Terms of Service guidelines:

> Participating successfully in newsgroups is a matter of common sense and common courtesy. Most AOL members are able to use their own sense of what is appropriate to guide their behavior. There will, however, always be innocent, inadvertent postings and there will also always be malicious, intentional postings. While it is not always clear which case is which, certain activities will result in an America Online member receiving a Terms of Service warning or more severe action. Postings that will result in Terms of Service actions include the following: . . . Inappropriate Posts. Each newsgroup focuses on a particular set of topics. Posts not related to these topics are not appreciated by the participants. It is important that America Online members become familiar with the culture and guidelines of a particular newsgroup before posting. Doing so will make your experience with newsgroups much more pleasant.

The culture and guidelines of most newsgroups/mailing lists involve topics in which all members agree (or, at least, agree to disagree). Getting on a list simply to disagree with these topics is not appropriate. People on AOL have been known to lose their accounts over such matters. But, in a more minor sense, AOL members have received a horrible reputation on the Net due to people like yourself promoting others not to follow Netiquette. As I suggested at the start, please consider making a correction to your suggestion in the same publication in which this was printed.

Shari

Dear Shari:

May we dispense with idle threats, please? As Queen Victoria put it, "We are not amused." Nowhere is there an Internet provision that states that it is inappropriate to get on a list if one happens to disagree with much that is said on the list. If it turns out that a disagreeing person becomes disagreeable, the moderator of the list has power to unsubscribe him [drop him from membership].

Please note that the passage you quoted says that inappropriate posts are those that are not related to the topic of a list. In *This Rock* have we suggested that people subscribe to Sister-L and then start posting dinner recipes or train schedules? No, we think they should talk about the subject of the list, which happens to be the religious life.

You say "the culture and guidelines of [lists] involve topics in which all members agree (or, at least, agree to disagree)." Well, it seems your last phrase fits the situation perfectly. If people follow our suggestion, they will find themselves probably disagreeing with posts on Sister-L, but there's every reason to suspect they will be quite agreeable in doing so. (Remember, these are people who think that uncharitableness not only is unsocial but is, in the plainest terms, sinful, and they believe they need to confess their sins with some regularity—an act no one enjoys, and the prospect of it militates against committing sins.)

I find your implications unsettling. I have subscribed to several lists that have been denominated as orthodox Catholic, yet these lists freely welcome both heterodox Catholics and non-Catholics, even anti-Catholics. Why? Because the orthodox actually believe that open discussion is a good thing. How is it, then, that those at the other end of the theological spectrum, despite words to the contrary, so often act as though the only speech they welcome is speech that agrees with them?

Karl Keating

To: KKeating

Interesting citation [to *Casablanca*], but I do not see the relationship to my statements. Perhaps we differ on what the stakes are in respecting the dialogue fostered by Sister-L. We will let Mr. Fox speak for himself. However, I find it hard to imagine that he was inviting those who do not agree with his opinions to launch a campaign to disrupt the lists he mentions.

Again, I do not see the relevance of your comments [about the U.N. and W.H.O.] to Sister-L. I prefer not to speak by innuendo but openly and in plain terms, so that honest misunderstandings can be cleared up. The Gospels and civilized morality have principles which apply to our respect for one another and to our equality as human beings. The U.N. General Assembly and the World Health Organization do not have anything to do with my point: Let Sister-L alone unless you have something to offer within its statement of purpose.

Here is where we differ: Sister-L does not apply litmus tests. If you re-read my message, you will note that I object to your prejudgment that Sister-L is heterodox. I doubt if there is enough data in Sister-L's archives to give you even a random sample of opinions as a sufficient base for a scientific application of your litmus tests. Note that we are not discussing actual or possible forums. We are discussing one list that does exist and has a real history of a few months. It has one negative prescription: Bashing of sisters is unwelcome. If anyone finds your list of heresies relevant to the purposes of Sister-L discussion, they [sic] are free to speak of the matters. Many of us are scholars and discuss all kinds of heresies in other contexts.

Discussion does not imply adherence to the positions discussed. For example, the sin of sexism condemned recently by the American bishops might come up for discussion. I believe this sin is related to the heresy that the unknowable God is male. This might conceivably be discussed on Sister-L in relation to the history and present concerns of women religious.

I do not find it in conformity with the basic teachings of the Gospel and of the Church to take on oneself the prerogative of labeling others as heretics, nor do I grant to other self-appointed interpreters of orthodoxy that right. Heresy is a serious matter. The first requirement for such a judgment is for the authorities to read the writings of the accused. Remember, we are discussing Sister-L, not some mythical forum of your imagination. You are not invited to serve as the grand inquisitor for Sister-L.

[You wrote,] "I must say, as I said in my reply to Prof. Thompson's message, that I am pleased to learn that you think it is a smear to accuse someone of being a feminist. This, at least, is encouraging." Neither Professor Thompson or myself have said that, and you know it. I have called myself a feminist for some twenty or more years.

Do we have nothing in common, such as the Gospel imperative to love? I do, as a feminist, believe in male-female mutuality. Perhaps we part company on this theme. In summary, Sister-L has its own agenda and will pursue that agenda. If you do not approve of it (presuming you know anything about it), turn to other matters. But do not make Sister-L into a phantom enemy which you imagine to be a threat to all your cherished belief.

Ritamary Bradley

Sr. Bradley:

You have confirmed my intuition. You admit Sister-L has an agenda. This is not surprising, of course. If you suspect that Mr. Fox was not inviting those who disagree with him or with the thrust of Sister-L, you accuse him of not encouraging an open and free dialogue. Now you may be right about his thinking—I can't speak to that, not knowing him or having asked him—but I am disappointed that you evince no dismay at such an attitude.

Have I labeled any subscriber to Sister-L a heretic? No. How can I, since I don't even know who subscribes, aside from the people who have written to me? Have I labeled some opinions as heterodox? Yes. Please keep in mind that in the Catholic Church we profess a common faith when we recite the creed, and this faith is explicated in the decrees of ecumenical councils, in the statements of popes, and most recently in *The Catechism of the Catholic Church*. To the extent one disagrees with the beliefs taught by the Church, one is heterodox. This heterodoxy might be quite innocent, in which case it can't be termed heresy. If the disagreement is on a matter of doctrine, is made with full knowledge that it does not conform to official Church teaching, is public, and is pertinacious, then it qualifies as heresy—or heresy has no meaning at all.

But again: I have called no one a heretic, not just with respect to Sister-L, but in the pages of *This Rock*, in public lectures, or in any other forum, so please do not insinuate that I have. I am careful to distinguish between the status of a belief (whether or not it accords with Church teaching) and the status of an individual.

You ask, "Do we have nothing in common, such as the Gospel imperative to love?" Of course we do, and we are obliged to follow that imperative, and it includes the obligation to love not only one another but to love the truth, which ultimately means to love Jesus Christ, who is the way, the truth, and the life.

Karl Keating

Mr. Keating:

I am one of the charter members and a member of the advisory board of Sister-L. I invite you to read the list for a time. I think you would find conversation of quality, intelligence, and real concern for the church. The subscribers—religious women, men, and people without public vows—engage in wide-ranging discussions on a variety of topics. We refrain from the kind of mean-spirited, ill-informed remarks you made in your publication.

Regina Siegfried, ASC
Aquinas Institute of Theology,
St. Louis, Missouri

Prof. Siegfried:

I would be delighted to have my initial suspicion proved false. I am thinking of subscribing under the *nom de plume* (not *nom de guerre*!) of HildegardB.

Karl Keating

To: KKeating

I don't know what you read as threats because none of my message was intended to be a threat. But I do hope none of the people who read your message are on commercial services where they can lose their accounts. The people of the Internet are not very friendly toward AOLers to begin with and really can't stand ones who don't abide by the rules of Netiquette.

People threatened to complain about my post on a newsgroup about dogs because I dared to mention that I wanted to breed my dog. I found out later that the newsgroup I was on was against breeding. I should have read the information about the list first, so that was my mistake. I also inadvertently posted an offer for a free catalog on a list where I saw advertisements. I didn't realize I was posting in the wrong place. Again, I should have read before posting to determine the culture and guidelines of the list. For this, I received a strict warning from the AOL staff.

I've learned much since I first started posting on the Internet. I have learned the hard way, and my message to you was simply warning you of the possibilities that lie ahead if you post messages as you describe in your message. If you are going into these mailing lists to read and learn, I am all for it. But if you are going in to convert or to try and prove that people are wrong, it is a complete misuse of the Net, and I hope you don't lose your AOL account over it.

Shari Vogt

Miss Vogt:

If people on that dog list threatened to complain about you for posting a single message about breeding your dog, you were the victim of illiberal minds. It's one thing to keep commercial messages in fixed locations—we can agree that such restrictions might be needed—but it's something else to come down heavily on someone for innocently posting a message.

You advise joining a list if one wishes to read and learn. But that presupposes that on the list there are other people who teach, right? I hope you will concur that we all can be teachers and learners at once, and this is why I encourage people to subscribe to lists (of whatever sort). Yes, they can be readers and learners, but they also can be writers and teachers so that others may be readers and learners. Call it reciprocity, if you will.

Karl Keating

To: KKeating

But the problem, Karl, is that your idea of teaching, from what I gather from your message in *The Rock* [sic] (please correct me if I am wrong) is not teaching, but converting. You are asking people who disagree completely with the intentions of a list to sign on and use it as a means of witnessing. No matter how much you disagree with me or with Netiquette, that is an inappropriate use of the Net.

Shari Vogt

Miss Vogt:

I seem to be receiving mixed signals from founders and members of Sister-L. By some I'm told that there is no party line on the list, but you advise that people who disagree completely with the intentions of a list shouldn't participate in it. But if the intention of Sister-L is to discuss the religious life, then it seems that anyone willing to discuss that topic, no matter from what angle, should be welcome.

On the other hand, if the discussion is expected to proceed along only one point of view, namely the feminist, then it appears that some members of the list are trying to mislead me or have been guilty of false advertising. I think you and I both know what the real story is, and I will not ask you to place yourself in an awkward position by continuing this exchange. Please know that you have my best regards and my thanks for your civility.

Karl Keating

7

No Apology from the New Apologists

On April 15, 1997, at St. John's Seminary in Camarillo, California (Archdiocese of Los Angeles), I gave the final lecture in a four-part series on apologetics. My predecessors were Rev. Robert Barron, assistant professor of philosophy and theology at Mundelein Seminary; Bishop Stephen E. Blaire, auxiliary bishop of Los Angeles; and Thomas P. Rausch, S.J., professor of theological studies at Loyola Marymount University. Speaking two months before me, Fr. Rausch used his lecture to blast "the new apologists," and he named names: Scott and Kimberly Hahn, Peter Kreeft, Dale Vree, Thomas Howard, the late Sheldon Vanauken. He reserved a disproportionate amount of his ire for me. Naturally enough, his comments forced me to modify the focus of my remarks, which were to be on how to respond to the Fundamentalist challenge. Below is the text that I delivered.

To be assigned the last slot in a lecture series carries advantages and disadvantages. You have the luxury of the last word and, if necessary, the consolation of having a chance to explain and defend yourself—something I propose to do momentarily—but you also find that your theme and possibly even your style have been determined for you by your predecessors. This I unhappily learned last year. I brought to a conference a typescript about which I was especially proud. My remarks were framed—rather cleverly, I thought—in the style of C. S. Lewis's *Screwtape Letters*. Imagine my dismay when a preceding speaker, Peter Kreeft, used the same motif for his remarks. I realized at once that I would be unable to trump him—the letter I had composed was supposedly from an apprentice tempter, but his was from Lucifer himself. I was forced to discard my typescript and speak extemporaneously.

I do not feel in such desperate straits today, yet I find that my topic, which concerns the proper way to deal with Protestant Fundamentalism, already has been reshaped in part by each of the three preceding speakers. It is unnecessary for me to pass along ground already trod by them. I propose, therefore, to emphasize not so much the necessity of evangelization, as delineated in *Redemptoris Missio* and *Ut Unum Sint*, but rather the very legitimacy of the evangelization movement that has developed in large part in response to the success enjoyed by Fundamentalists who have sought to pull Catholics from the religion of their upbringing. Today this movement is by no means restricted to dealing with the Fundamentalist challenge, although, ten years ago, that was its chief focus. Today the movement, almost entirely lay-run, attempts to explain Catholicism not just to self-styled "Bible Christians," but to people of no particular religion and even to those many Catholics who are unsure of their own faith or who rebel against it.

Two of my predecessors in this series, Bishop Stephen E. Blaire and Fr. Thomas P. Rausch, have used the term "new apologetics" to label this movement. One might begin by noting that this is not a new label. The phrase "a new apologetic" was used by Msgr. Ronald Knox as the subtitle to his never-completed book *Proving God*,[1] which he worked on more than forty years ago, and even then the phrase was not new. It was used by Catholic apologists of the twenties and thirties, the heyday of the Catholic Evidence Guild, to label an apologetic movement that sought to deal with questions that actually were on the minds of non-Catholic inquirers (as distinguished from questions that were only in the minds of textbook writers).

Looked at one way, the term "new apologetics" conveys barely more than chronology: It is the latest form of apologetics, whatever form that might be. Using this connotation it would be right to say that at one time Justin Martyr engaged in the new apologetics. Later, Augustine was a new apologist, as were Thomas Aquinas,

---

[1] Ronald A. Knox, *Proving God* (London, *The Month*, n.d.).

Robert Bellarmine, and, in this country, Orestes Brownson and Isaac Hecker. But this merely chronological connotation empties the term of useful meaning and is not really the sense in which the term is used today—at least not by those who publicly oppose what they label "the new apologetics."

Of course, not everyone uses the term pejoratively; in these remarks I will use it neutrally. But those who do use it pejoratively designate by it something they consider wrong-headed and possibly dangerous. They think that the new apologists not only have an unnuanced understanding of the Catholic faith and little familiarity with modern Catholic theologizing but that their methodologies are ineffective or even counterproductive. Some of the critics fear that the new apologists will injure ecumenical relations. Others worry that the new apologists will sap their own work of needed vitality. (They do not say this in so many words, but this seems to be a major concern.)

Some opponents of the new apologetics cite the conclusion of a study prepared for the American bishops' Ad Hoc Committee on Proselytism. The study concluded that there "is little empirical evidence" to support the theory that one of the key reasons for defections "is proselytism on the part of other churches." On the contrary, other churches "may be attracting Catholics because of their warm evangelization, rather than because of coercive techniques."[2]

This sets up a straw man. Coercive techniques are almost never used when Catholics are proselytized. Mormons, Jehovah's Witnesses, and self-described "Bible Christians" twist no arms, make no threats, suggest no violence. On the other hand, Catholics do not leave the Church of their upbringing solely because these other churches carry on "warm evangelization"—that is, they do not leave solely for social or emotional reasons. Such reasons may move them to investigate these other churches—encouragement by a Fundamentalist neighbor may induce a Catholic to attend a Bible

---

[2] Eleace King, *Proselytism and Evangelization: An Exploratory Study* (Georgetown: Georgetown University, 1991), 16.

study, for example—but Catholics do not join these churches unless they subscribe to their distinctive doctrinal positions. No one becomes a Mormon unless he believes in the historicity of Joseph Smith's revelations. No one becomes a Jehovah's Witness unless he concludes that Jesus Christ is not divine and that hell does not exist. No one becomes a Fundamentalist unless he holds that the Bible is the sole rule of faith.

The process that brings Catholics out of the Church and into other religions almost always includes appeals to the intellect. Call these appeals what you will—proselytism, proof texting, or just plain arguing—the appeals work, and they work because they are couched in terms of the duty of Catholics to apply reason to their faith. These Catholics, many of them habitual Mass-goers, have received little intellectual sustenance from their parishes. They are effectively uncatechized. In not a few cases they have been *de*catechized: Private doubts have been thrust upon them, and they quietly wonder why they should remain in a church whose leaders issue contradictory messages from the pulpit and in the confessional.

So how should we deal with Catholics who are on their way out of the Church and with people who are encouraging them to leave and to join "Bible believing" churches? And how should we deal with those Catholics, even more numerous, who are not tempted to join such churches but who simply fall away from the active practice of the faith or who reject portions of it?

Bishop Blaire suggests that "the proper modality for apologetics as we enter the new millennium is one of persuasion through dialogue."[3] In this I believe he is exactly right, and this happens to be the approach that the new apologists have been using with considerable effect. The dialogue may be conducted privately, over a considerable period of time, or publicly, in a single evening. It need not be oral; it may be in the form of letters, pamphlets,

---

[3] Most Rev. Stephen E. Blaire, "The Apologetic Moment in Evangelization" (given at St. John's Seminary, Camarillo, California, on December 3, 1996), 9.

or books. It may be conducted across the airwaves. Recently it has been conducted through e-mail and in Internet newsgroups. However it is manifested, it consists in a reciprocal sharing of perspectives, of beliefs, of differences—always, one hopes, in an atmosphere of charity.

While I concur with Bishop Blaire in the necessity of dialogue, I must demur when he says that "[r]esearch suggests that it is not theological argument which is going to bring people back."[4] I find the research to which he alludes[5] faulty in that it does not take into account the testimony of those who actually engage in apologetics as a vocation or a profession. Our experience is all to the contrary: Theological argument, while not a universal salve, has brought many back to the Church or into the Church for the first time. This is especially true of former Fundamentalists, many of whom once were Catholic, many of whom never were Catholic but were nourished on anti-Catholic prejudices. I have yet to meet a Fundamentalist-turned-Catholic who came into the Church without engaging in—and without expecting to be engaged in—argumentation. Nearly always, in fact, it is the Fundamentalist who brings up disputed points, long before he has any suspicion that the Catholic faith is an option for him.

True, no one can be argued into faith, but the act of faith may be impossible for those whose way to the Church is strewn with stumbling blocks. The apologist's task is to remove the stumbling blocks or, at least, to help inquirers see around them. Are popes sinners? Indeed, as are we all, but the inquirer needs to learn that the absence of papal impeccability tells us nothing about the existence of papal infallibility. Do Catholics worship Mary? Of course not, but it is not enough to wave one's hand dismissively, as though the question is beneath consideration. The charge must be answered as forthrightly as it is made. To do less is to show little respect for the non-Catholic, who, understandably enough,

---

[4] Ibid., 15.

[5] Dean R. Hoge, *Converts, Dropouts, Returnees* (Cleveland: Pilgrim Press, 1981).

will go away thinking that an unanswered question is an unanswerable question.

I agree with Bishop Blaire that, in the case of fallen-away Catholics, all that may be necessary for a resumption of active participation in the Church is a friendly invitation to return to Mass and the sacraments. Sometimes it surprises one to see how little coaxing it takes to bring the lethargic to their spiritual senses. But a mere invitation is never enough if we are dealing with Catholics who have difficulties or doubts about what the Church teaches on faith or morals, or with Christians who belong to other churches precisely because they disagree with Catholic beliefs, or with the unchurched, who will see no point in accepting an invitation if they cannot take Christianity seriously in the first place.

Many people harbor a fear of controversy. Dialogue is fine, they say, so long as there is little focus on differences. Nothing good can come from argument, no matter how civilly it may be conducted. But such an attitude strips dialogue of its usefulness. A disinclination to argue about differences implies a lack of respect for the other person, an unwillingness to consider his views important. As Rabbi Jacob Neusner has written, "[W]e can argue only if we take one another seriously . . . [W]e can enter into dialogue only if we honor both ourselves and the other."[6] If we are unwilling to deal with Fundamentalists and others on their own terms, we should not be surprised if we see little ecumenical progress being made with them. However necessary it is for scholars to work in remote acreages of the mind—and undoubtedly that is necessary —we avoid an authentically ecumenical engagement if we decline to fashion an apologetic that approaches people on a popular level and treats their concerns seriously. It is likely that no one has ever been brought from atheism to theism merely by an application of Aquinas's five proofs, and it is equally likely that no one has ever been brought from nominal Christianity to fervent Christianity by a deconstruction of biblical texts.

---

[6] Jacob Neusner, *A Rabbi Talks with Jesus* (New York: Doubleday, 1993), xii.

The new apologists are criticized for harboring skepticism regarding some of today's theologizing. Fr. Rausch says, "Whatever their primary motivation, these new apologists are deeply suspicious of modern scholarship."[7] He sees "a lack of sympathy for mainstream Roman Catholic theology."[8] The new apologists suffer from "an inability to reconcile faith with critical reason,"[9] and they "appear unable to enter into a real dialogue with modernity, with the critical questions it raises for faith."[10]

If I may be so bold as to criticize these comments, I would note first that "contemporary Catholic theology" is not of one cloth. William May is not Charles Curran. Joseph Ratzinger is not Edward Schillebeeckx. Bernard Orchard is not Raymond Brown. Each of these men is a Catholic theologian writing today, and thus each produces "contemporary Catholic theology." If the new apologists are unsympathetic to the thought of the second man in each pairing, it is no more and no less accurate to say that the opponents of the new apologists are unsympathetic to the thought of the first man in each pairing. Thus, it would be equally accurate —and equally meaningless—for the new apologists to say of their detractors that they are unsympathetic to that half of "contemporary Catholic theology" which is the one more closely aligned with the thought of John Paul II.

Fr. Rausch claims that the new apologists "are relentlessly hostile to contemporary Catholic theology precisely because it is critical."[11] This is incorrect, on two grounds. The new apologists use much contemporary Catholic theology, such as that produced by Hans Urs von Balthasar, Henri de Lubac, Avery Dulles, Aidan Nichols, and even Francis Sullivan (the latter with occasional reservations, admittedly). To the extent the new apologists are "hos-

---

[7] Thomas P. Rausch, S.J., "Apologetics or Evangelization?" (given at St. John's Seminary, Camarillo, California, on February 4, 1997), 8.

[8] Ibid., 9.

[9] Ibid., 13.

[10] Ibid.

[11] Ibid., 13.

tile" to "contemporary Catholic theology," their "hostility" is either to heterodoxy, as exemplified in the promotion of priestly ordination for women or in the rejection of *Humanae Vitae*, or to poorly reasoned positions, such as those adduced in favor of the late dating of the New Testament books.

Let us grant that "hostility" toward some "contemporary Catholic theology" exists (though I think it might better be described as "skepticism"). What is the origin of it? Fr. Rausch says the new apologists dislike what he identifies as mainstream theology because it is critical and they are not. But much of that theology is critical only in a certain sense. It is critical in that it criticizes what has been the received teaching or understanding. But it is often quite uncritical when looking at itself.

One of its greatest failings—and this is shown most especially in biblical studies—is that many scholars have misappropriated the methodology of statistics and frame their arguments in terms of probabilities. Probabilities are piled upon probabilities, with little appreciation that, as intermediate probabilities multiply, the final probability rapidly shrinks in size, often to the point of impossibility. Something that is "more likely than not" is said to be dependent upon something that "in all likelihood is so," which in turn arises out of something else that is "nearly certain." In the hands of these exegetes, the result is not what a mathematician would expect—virtually zero—but instead is hailed as one of the "assured results of modern critical scholarship." As J. A. Baird has noted: "[O]ne has only to pick up almost any commentary and read at random: 'without a doubt,' 'there can be no question,' 'it is obvious that,' 'it is absolutely certain.' There is no field of human thought further from scientific discipline, at this moment, than that of biblical exegesis."[12]

Credulity has never been considered a virtue, except by those who have a stake in it. Far more blameworthy than a reluctance to embrace uncritically all aspects of modern theology is the fear,

---

[12] J. A. Baird, *Audience Criticism and the Historical Jesus* (Philadelphia: Westminster, 1969), 30.

shown by some theologians, of the truly innovative or revolution-
ary.

Consider the reception given to men engaged not in parroting
doctoral dissertations but in producing original work. In 1976 appeared John A. T. Robinson's *Redating the New Testament*. Robinson, an Anglican bishop, could not be accused of being a conservative. It was his 1963 book, *Honest to God*, that ushered in the
self-styled New Morality. In *Redating the New Testament* he said he
wanted to take a fresh look at the evidence for dating the books
of the New Testament. He said, "Indeed what one looks for in
vain in much recent scholarship is any serious wrestling with the
external or internal evidence for the dating of individual books
. . . rather than an *a priori* pattern of theological development into
which they are then made to fit."[13] Robinson cited Norman Per-
rin as a good bad example of this tendency.

Robinson noted that no book of the New Testament mentions
the fall of Jerusalem, which occurred in A.D. 70, as a past fact.
"[T]he silence is . . . as significant as the silence for Sherlock
Holmes of the dog that did not bark."[14] Robinson concludes that
the Gospel of Matthew could have been written as early as the
year 40 and that Revelation probably was written not at the close
of the century but in 68.

When Robinson's argument was not pooh-poohed by the critics,
it was ignored. Similarly with the later argument of Claude Tresmontant, professor at the Sorbonne. He concluded that Matthew's
Gospel as we have it, in Greek, must have been a translation of
an original in Hebrew, and that original must have been written
no later than the year 40 and possibly within a year of the Resurrection of Christ—similarly with the other Gospels.[15] Tresmontant too was shunted aside, as was Jean Carmignac, a Dead Sea

---

[13] John A. T. Robinson, *Redating the New Testament* (Philadelphia: Westminster, 1976), 8–9.

[14] Ibid., 13.

[15] Claude Tresmontant, *The Hebrew Christ* (Chicago: Franciscan Herald,
1989).

Scrolls translator. He used a distinctive analysis that he described as "principally philological but also historical on occasion," as distinguished from Robinson's methodology, which he termed "exclusively historical," and Tresmontant's, which he termed "partially historical and partially philological."[16] Carmignac also concluded that the synoptics were written first in Hebrew and only later were translated into Greek.

Among his arguments was this startling one concerning the Benedictus, which appears in Luke 1:68–79. In the first line of the second strophe is the verb *hânan*, which is the root of the name John. In the second line is the verb *zâkar*, which is the root of the name Zachary. In the third line is the verb *shâba*, which is the root of the name Elizabeth. This triple allusion to the three protagonists appears only if our Greek text is "translated backward" into Hebrew; it does not appear in Greek or in English.[17]

Like Robinson, like Tresmontant, Carmignac was tut-tutted off stage. He had declined to acquiesce to the reigning orthodoxy. He was authentically critical in his research, and the sorry fact is that many theologians—and this is especially true of biblical scholars—are not really very scientific in their work. They are weak where physical scientists tend to be strong. Scientists tend to be ruthlessly self-critical, and they reject hypotheses that fail to stand up to tests to which they have been subjected. The problem with some modern theology is not just that it fails to entertain contrary views but that it persists in holding hypotheses "in favor of which solid and satisfactory evidence has never been adduced."[18] A good example of this is the supposed existence of the document Q, without which the theory of Markan priority would collapse. No external evidence for Q has ever been located—Papias's *Logia* does not really qualify. The argument for Q's existence depends

---

[16] Jean Carmignac, *The Birth of the Synoptics* (Chicago: Franciscan Herald, 1987), 86.

[17] Ibid., 27–28.

[18] Stephen Neill, *The Interpretation of the New Testament 1861–1961* (London: Oxford, 1966), 346.

on the Gospels' internal evidence, of which there is very little. A great edifice has been built upon Q. The structure and dating of the Gospels are said to be dependent on Q. If so, then Q is the most important document of Christian antiquity, yet no writer in antiquity seems to have heard of it.

In college, in a history of science course, we studied the Ptolemaic theory in detail. We used the celestial measurements taken down by the ancients and worked out the complex mathematical formulas, and we demonstrated how the sun, the planets, and the stars orbited the earth along cycles and epicycles. There was great beauty and deep satisfaction in the way that the Ptolemaic theory, to use the medieval expression, "saved the appearances"—that is, the way it accounted for observations taken by the naked eye. The theory even explained the retrograde motion of some of the planets. Then we turned to the more precise measurements taken by Tycho Brahe in the late sixteenth century; his observations of the planets formed the basis for Kepler's laws of planetary motion. We saw that the Ptolemaic theory had trouble accommodating the new data. Once the telescope was invented a few decades after Brahe's time, measurements became still more precise, and it became obvious that the Ptolemaic theory no longer worked, no longer "saved the appearances," and it collapsed. It was a magnificent theory, one on which many scholarly reputations depended, but it disappeared overnight. I often think of the Ptolemaic theory when I think of the theory of Markan priority and Q and how that modern theory is being undermined by advances in biblical knowledge. I would not be surprised to see the latter theory supplanted as quickly as the former was.

The New Jerome Biblical Commentary dates Matthew's Gospel between A.D. 80 and 90 and more likely toward the end of that decade.[19] This seems to be the received opinion, but it is being challenged today not just by the exegetes I have mentioned,

---

[19] Benedict V. Viviano, "The Gospel According to Matthew" in *The New Jerome Biblical Commentary*, Raymond E. Brown, S.S., et al., eds. (Englewood Cliffs: Prentice Hall, 1990), 631.

but from another direction, that of papyrology. At the end of 1994 Carsten Thiede, a papyrologist who directs the Institute for Basic Epistemological Research in Paderborn, Germany, announced his findings concerning three papyrus scraps belonging to Magdalen College, Oxford. The scraps contain phrases from the twenty-sixth chapter of Matthew's Gospel. A few decades earlier the scraps had been dated as coming from the end of the second century and therefore were thought uninteresting and were forgotten, but Thiede, literally taking a fresh look by using a newly invented high-power microscope, concluded that the dating was faulty. He said the scraps were written no later than the year 60, which is to say about three decades earlier than the date given in *The New Jerome Biblical Commentary*. As *The Times* of London said, the finding "provides the first material evidence that the Gospel according to St. Matthew is an eyewitness account written by contemporaries of Christ."[20]

If Thiede's finding is accurate—or if the conclusions of Robinson, Tresmontant, or Carmignac are borne out—much recent biblical scholarship will have to be rethought—as, in many quarters, it is being rethought anyway. This is a prospect many contemporary scholars fear, since their life's work would be proved valueless: Nothing has less currency than a passé theory. The trauma would be comparable to that suffered, in the eighteenth century, by believers in phlogiston, who saw their writings become worthless when the oxygen theory of combustion was promulgated.

Thus it appears that it may not be the new apologists who are uncritical in their positions. It may be that their opinions will be, in a few years' time, in considerably greater favor than the ones now preferred by their opponents. With that prospect in mind, perhaps I need not take too seriously Fr. Rausch's complaint that I take "the Bread of Life Discourse in John 6 as the historical words of Jesus rather than as the Eucharistic theology of the Johannine

---

[20] Carsten Peter Thiede and Matthew D'Ancona, *Eyewitness to Jesus* (New York: Doubleday, 1996), 1.

community."[21] I plead *nolo contendere*, since I think the evidence points to an early date for the composition of John's Gospel—at least thirty years earlier than generally thought—and, if so, John must have been the author of the Gospel attributed to him. There would have been no time for any "Johannine community" to arise and to embellish his writings. Thus the words attributed to Jesus in John 6 are likely to be his *ipsissima verba*, not just his *ipsissima vox*.

By the way, we must be cautious in attributing much to these communities. As admitted in *The New Jerome Biblical Commentary*'s discussion of the composition of John's Gospel, these communities are hypotheses, mere theoretical constructs built up from evaluations of the internal structure of the books in question.[22] There is scant evidence for the communities outside of the New Testament. Martin Hengel's judgment was that these "community constructions" often seem to be modern fabrications rather than historical realities.[23]

However that may be, I am reminded of the salutary words written by A. H. N. Green-Armytage nearly fifty years ago:

> There is a world—I do not say a world in which all scholars live but one at any rate into which all of them sometimes stray, and which some of them seem permanently to inhabit—which is not the world in which I live. In my world, if *The Times* and *The Telegraph* both tell one story in somewhat different terms, nobody concludes that one of them must have copied the other, nor that the variations in the story have some esoteric significance. But in that world of which I am speaking this would be taken for granted. There, no story is ever derived from facts but always from somebody else's version of the same story. . . . In my world, almost every book, except some of those produced by Government departments, is written by one author. In that world almost every book is produced by a

---

[21] Rausch, 17.

[22] Pheme Perkins, "The Gospel According to John" in *The New Jerome Biblical Commentary* (Englewood Cliffs: Prentice Hall, 1990), 945-946.

[23] Martin Hengel, *Acts and the History of the Earliest Christians*, John Bowden trans. (London: SCM Press, 1979), 25.

committee, and some of them by a whole series of committees. In my world, if I read that Mr. Churchill, in 1935, said that Europe was heading for a disastrous war, I applaud his foresight. In that world no prophecy, however vaguely worded, is ever made except after the event. In my world we say, "The First World War took place in 1914–1918." In that world they say, "The world-war narrative took shape in the third decade of the twentieth century." In my world men and women live for a considerable time—seventy, eighty, even a hundred years—and they are equipped with a thing called memory. In that world (it would appear) they come into being, write a book, and forthwith perish, all in a flash, and it is noted of them with astonishment that they "preserve traces of primitive tradition" about things which happened well within their own adult lifetime.[24]

Then there is the stinging indictment that the new apologists like old books. I have been chided, for example, for recommending the 1914 *Catholic Encyclopedia* over the 1967 *New Catholic Encyclopedia*.[25] In most cases, I think, I am right to do so. The original edition has a third again as many pages, and those pages are set in considerably smaller type. Admittedly, that edition covers fifty fewer years than does the later one, but the difference in format and the missing half century mean that it covers many topics that are not covered at all in the second edition, and those that are covered in both editions are usually covered in much greater depth in the original. I discovered this when writing *Catholicism and Fundamentalism*. The 1967 edition of the encyclopedia has scant information on Bishop Josip Strossmayer, to whom is attributed, falsely, an anti-papal speech said to have been given at Vatican I. The speech is not even mentioned in the 1967 edition. The 1914 edition's article on Strossmayer is twice as long and discusses the forgery.

Not only have I been chided for using an encyclopedia written before I was born but for recommending a book written by a bib-

---

[24] A. H. N. Green-Armytage, *John Who Saw* (1952), 12, quoted in Robinson, 356.

[25] Rausch, 10.

lical scholar who has the effrontery to believe in the historicity of the infancy narratives.[26] In my reveries I imagine a clerical figure, looking somewhat like Claude Rains in *Casablanca*, saying, "I am shocked—shocked I say—to learn that a contemporary Catholic scholar believes what no Catholic scholar doubted until the late twentieth century."

I once knew a deacon who had succumbed to the sin of chronological snobbery. He refused to read any religion book written before 1965, the year that Vatican II ended. Nothing that came before was any longer of value, he said. I did not embarrass him by asking whether he read the Bible. If one were to be so foolish as to mark a date as a cutoff for reading, surely it would be prudent, if choosing 1965, to forswear reading books published later rather than earlier. It is better to give up Hans Küng for Karl Adam, Joyce Carol Oates for Flannery O'Connor, Maya Angelou for Dante Alighieri. The deacon forgot—or maybe never knew —that whoever marries the spirit of the age will be widowed in the next.

But one does not have to make such a choice, and the new apologists do not make it. In their work they draw from the latest Catholic writers, such as John Paul II and Joseph Ratzinger, and from the oldest, such as Cyprian and Irenaeus. The new apologists are the only ones, so far as I can see, who, in popular writings and lectures, regularly quote the Fathers of the Church. They are engaged not just in a theoretical but in a practical *ressourcement*. With T. S. Eliot they firmly believe that the dead have something to say to us and that "the communication of the dead is tongued with fire beyond the language of the living."[27]

I recall speaking at a parish in Los Angeles some years ago and recommending patristic writings to my listeners. That evening our book table sold thirty three-volume sets of the writings of the Fathers. Those sets, which sold for forty-five dollars apiece, were

---

[26] Ibid.

[27] T. S. Eliot, "Little Gidding" in *The Complete Poems and Plays 1909–1950* (New York: Harcourt, Brace & World, 1952), 139.

purchased by everyday Catholics who had just been reminded that their faith was not born in 1965 but is two thousand years old. I wonder how many students taught by critics of the new apologetics ever purchase the writings of the Fathers—other than when forced to buy a pocketbook edition for classroom use?

This brings us to a recurring argument of the opponents of the new apologetics. The new apologists must be wrong because, as Fr. Rausch says, "[m]ost theologians would disagree"[28] with them. But this is facile. As David R. Hall notes,

> The fact that a line of inquiry begun by Scholar A was developed by a hundred scholars in the next generation does not make that line of inquiry more valid than that of Scholar B whose work is almost forgotten. Scholar A's work was certainly fruitful in the propagation of doctoral theses but *not necessarily* in the propagation of truth.[29]

We are to believe that, if "most theologians" hold a position on a certain issue, the position must be true. That's flabby thinking. Recall the movie *Twelve Angry Men*. It was about how one juror held out for acquittal, turned out to be right, and eventually convinced the other eleven. No one watching that movie would have thought it good if the lone juror had decided to go along with the others merely because "most jurors" initially believed in the defendant's guilt. Keep in mind that theologians do not enjoy the charism of infallibility. At times "most theologians" simply are wrong about a particular point. We need to examine the point itself, not take a hand count.

Along these lines Henri de Lubac wrote about an incident in the life of Paul Claudel, the French statesman, poet, and playwright. In 1907 Claudel received a letter from Jacques Riviere, "a young intellectual nearly destroyed by the pernicious philosophies of the day."[30] Riviere wrote, "I can see that Christianity is dying. . . .

---

[28] Rausch, 18.

[29] David R. Hall, *The Seven Pillories of Wisdom* (Macon: Mercer University, 1990), 5.

[30] Louis Chaigne, *Paul Claudel: The Man and the Mystic* (New York: Appleton-Century-Crofts, 1961), 108.

People no longer know why our towns are still surmounted by spires which are no longer the prayers of any of us; they don't know what is the point of those great buildings which are now hemmed in by railway stations and hospitals and from which the people themselves have expelled the monks; they don't know why the graveyards display pretentious stucco crosses of execrable design." De Lubac remarked, "And Claudel's answer to that cry of anguish was undoubtedly a good one: 'Truth is not concerned with how many people it convinces.' "[31]

If relying on numbers does not work, there are other arguments. If I may say so, I found it unhelpful that Fr. Rausch engaged in name calling (such as using "ultra conservative"[32] to describe William Most, a Scripture scholar with whom he disagrees). Regarding people who espoused a position he did not hold, Fr. Rausch said he "wonder[ed] if any of them have read and assimilated"[33] the relevant documents. He seemed unable to imagine that perhaps they had and had found good reasons not to draw his conclusions. It struck me as ungenerous for him to say that "some of the new apologists are genuinely concerned about the loss of Catholics"[34] to Fundamentalism and Evangelicalism. Only "some"? He forgets that the new apologists are the people who most often write and speak about this exodus out of the Church, and they are the only ones who have been successful in bringing former Catholics back in appreciable numbers.

Another complaint against the new apologists is that they engage in triumphalism—a curious word. It is what philosopher and rhetorician Richard Weaver called a "devil term." Such terms, he said, "defy any real analysis. That is to say, one cannot explain how they generate their peculiar force of repudiation. One only recog-

---

[31] Henri de Lubac, S.J., *The Drama of Atheist Humanism* (New York: Sheed & Ward, 1950), 69.

[32] Rausch, 10.

[33] Ibid., 14.

[34] Ibid., 32.

nizes them as publicly-agreed-upon devil terms."[35] It is enough to
call the new apologists triumphalistic: no need to define the term
or see if it fits. In what do they expect to triumph? In the Church
at the end of the world? Yes, at least in that. In the fact that many
people who fell away from the Church are now returning to it?
Yes, in that they are pleased. In their wish, found in Vatican II
and shared by every Catholic until just a few decades ago, that
non-Catholics might enjoy the fullness of Christian faith as found
only within the Catholic Church? Yes, even in that. But if that is
what triumphalism is, one should ask more fervently why those
opposed to the new apologetics wish to distance themselves from
these goals, which have been Catholic goals as long as there has
been a Catholic Church. Perhaps the perfervid use of epithets
such as "triumphalistic" tells us less about those against whom
the epithets are placed than about those who place the epithets.

I wonder: Can't we, in these internal squabbles, evince a little more charity? Can't we give the benefit of the doubt to fellow Catholics with whom we happen to disagree? Perhaps a little caution is in order on the part of those who dislike the new
apologetics. Although these strictures in Alexander Pope's *Essay
on Criticism* were addressed to literary critics, they seem applicable
to some of these other critics too:

> But you who seek to give and merit fame,
> And justly bear a Critic's noble name,
> Be sure yourself and your own reach to know,
> How far your genius, taste, and learning go;
> Launch not beyond your depth, but be discreet,
> And mark that point where sense and dullness meet.[36]

Each of my two immediate predecessors in this series made a
comment that seemed to me especially melancholy, though unin-

---

[35] Richard Weaver, *The Ethics of Rhetoric* (Chicago: Regnery, 1953), 222.

[36] Alexander Pope, "Essay in Criticism," in William K. Wimsatt, Jr., ed.,
Alexander Pope: Selected Poetry and Prose (New York: Holt, Rhinehart and Win-
ston, 1951), ll. 46–51.

tentionally so. Bishop Blaire remarked that "the NCCB Committee on Pastoral Practices has contracted with a liturgical and scriptural scholar to prepare reflections which incorporate the teaching of the *Catechism of the Catholic Church* into the Sunday homily, while maintaining the integrity of the homily"[37] as a reflection on the day's readings. I confess that I found this news disconcerting. Have we so declined that parish priests feel themselves incapable of composing good homilies without the supervision of a national committee? If so, then such supervision will not help them. A priest who has not already made the teaching of the Church his own cannot pass along that teaching by parroting the work of a lone "liturgical and scriptural scholar," even one chosen by the bishops.

Perhaps I am expecting too much in expecting priests to do their own homework and to draw their homilies out of their interior faith—but then I always have thought that presidents should give far fewer speeches and only those that they compose themselves. However effective the words of Ted Sorensen and Peggy Noonan, I still prefer the *ipsissima verba* of Washington and Lincoln. The Farewell Address and the Gettysburg Address are memorable not just because they are well written but because in them we see the souls of the speakers—something we have not seen in inaugural addresses for many decades. For a priest to catechize his congregation well, he first must be catechized himself, and a well-catechized priest will have little need for a national committee to oversee his homilies.

In what I found to be his most melancholy remark, Fr. Rausch said that, "after more than twenty years of teaching theology to undergraduates in a Roman Catholic University . . . the language in which we try to present the Good News doesn't have much meaning to many today, particularly to young adults."[38] He conceded that his theology and methodology fail to win minds or hearts. But the theology and methodology of the new apologists

---

[37] Blaire, 12.
[38] Ibid., 29–30.

actually work. At Catholic Answers, for instance, we can show visitors thousands of letters from college students and young adults who received no spiritual sustenance from their nominally Catholic universities but plenty from the kind of apologetics engaged in by the people Fr. Rausch castigates. He complains that "these new apologists will not be able to help contemporary Catholics develop a faith that is at once traditional and critical, able to withstand the challenges of secular modernity."[39] There is deep irony here in that it has been his own side that has "withstood" secular modernity by collapsing before it. Most of those allied with him cheerfully accept contraception as a positive good, they succumb to pop psychology fads, such as the enneagram, and from their ranks has come not a single major opponent of abortion.

One thinks of Milton, using, in *Lycidas*, an image from Dante's *Paradiso*:[40]

> The hungry Sheep look up, and are not fed,
> But swoln with wind, and the rank mist they draw,
> Rot inwardly, and foul contagion spread.[41]

How many young people have left nominally Catholic universities with their faith malnourished? How many of them have sought intellectual and spiritual sustenance from their religion courses only to find themselves, like the sheep, taking in nothing more substantial than air? Worse yet, how many of them "rot inwardly" and have gone on to spread confusions—or have forsaken the Catholic Church for another?

Joseph Priestly—the Unitarian philosopher and scientist who ended up being Hilaire Belloc's maternal great-great-grandfather —wrote in his *Memoirs* about a debate in Parliament regarding the Test Laws. Lord Sandwich, a naval man and not a theologian, said in frustration, "I have heard frequent use of the words 'orthodoxy'

---

[39] Ibid., 21–22.

[40] Dante Alighieri, *Paradiso* XXIX, ll. 106–107.

[41] John Milton, "Lycidas" in *John Milton: Complete Poems and Major Prose*, Merritt Y. Hughes, ed. (Indianapolis: Bobbs-Merrill, 1957), ll. 125–128.

and 'heterodoxy' but I confess myself at a loss to know precisely what they mean." William Warburton, the Anglican bishop of Gloucester, whispered to him, "Orthodoxy is my doxy; heterodoxy is another man's doxy."[42]

That's an engaging definition, but not an especially useful one. Let me propose an alternative for our use. It is simple, and it is old: Catholic orthodoxy consists of those teachings affirmed by the popes, and heterodoxy consists of contrary teachings. In our time, as in all times in Church history, truly critical minds and truly effective apologists will recognize that evangelization, if it is to be successful, must be based on right belief, and right belief cannot be reduced to a matter of individual preference or to a lazy acceptance of whichever "doxy" happens to be popular at the moment. From right belief will flow right action. In the absence of right belief, no right action will be forthcoming. No response to the Fundamentalist challenge—or to any other challenge, whether from outside or inside the Church—will prove fruitful unless it is grounded first in Catholic truth. No apologetic, whether denominated "new" or "old," will win hearts and minds unless it is rooted in doctrinal fidelity, spiritual transparency, and evident charity.

[42] Joseph Priestly, *Memoirs* I:572.

8

Upstart Theories

The synoptic problem is the chief detective story within New Testament scholarship. Are the first three Gospels—Matthew, Mark, and Luke—literarily dependent upon one another? They seem to be, since, when their text is arranged "synoptically" (with like verses next to one another in parallel columns), they seem to be saying the same things in more or less the same words and in more or less the same order. Many solutions have been proposed to account for the similarity—some solutions, such as Augustine's, being proposed before anyone realized the synoptic problem was a problem.

Frans Neirynck has been one of the leading "establishment" scholars in biblical scholarship and is a professor at the Catholic University of Leuven in Belgium. Since he is commonly cited as an authority on the question of the synoptics, we can look at his summary of the history of the solutions:

> The "Augustinian" hypothesis assumed the order of composition to be Matthew, Mark, Luke. For a period this was replaced as the leading theory by the Griesbach hypothesis (Matthew, Luke, Mark). The priority of Mark was first suggested at the end of the eighteenth century as an alternative to the traditional view of Matthean priority, leading to decisive debate in the 1830s to 1860s. As a result, the Markan hypothesis became the predominant scholarly opinion.

Quite true, but let's not draw the wrong conclusion. Markan priority remains the predominant opinion among professionals and, therefore, among amateurs who read and accept, often un-critically, what professionals say, but we shouldn't conclude willy-nilly that the hypothesis is correct. (We must keep in mind that

truth is not determined by a show of hands.) More and more scholars—though still a decided minority—are objecting to what has
been the scholarly consensus. Today we can see a move away from
Markan priority, coupled with a move away from late datings for
the Gospels.

I'd like to give an overview of three elements of the discussion:
the rise of the Markan priority hypothesis, the revival of the op-
posing Griesbach hypothesis, and the emerging influence of what
might be termed the "Hebrew Gospels" hypothesis. The reader
will come to see, I hope, that Markan priority, which is commonly termed an "assured result" of modern biblical scholarship,
is no longer a sure thing at all. (There are other variants in the
discussion, but to include them would make things unnecessarily
complicated. As it is, I must apologize for any lack of clarity in
what follows. I promise that the story gets clearer as we move
along.)

Neirynck says that

> the absence of Matthew-Luke agreement against Mark in terms of
> order can be interpreted in more than one way. It can be explained
> by Markan priority but also by any hypothesis that proposes Mark
> as a middle term. . . . But the real argument from order for Markan
> priority is that the differences in Matthew and Luke can be plau-
> sibly explained as changes of Mark made according to the general
> redactional [editorial] tendencies and the compositional purposes
> of each Gospel.

After charting the "Markan order in Matthew" and the "Markan
order in Luke," Neirynck presents the chief reason for holding
to Markan priority:

> We have discussed the common order of the Triple Tradition
> pericopes [short extracts] and have explained differences from the
> Markan order as "editorial divergences" by Matthew and Luke. The
> argument from order, as understood since Karl Lachmann (1835),
> constitutes the main reason for positing Markan priority.

But "our treatment of order suggesting the priority of Mark
as a solution to the synoptic problem is incomplete, for the non-

Markan material shared by Matthew and Luke is still to be considered." This material is thought to come from a source called "Q" (from the German *Quelle*, "source"). "Recent studies tend to confine Q material to (all the) passages attested in both Matthew and Luke. Too uncertain for consideration is the possibility that only Matthew or Luke preserved a passage from Q."

Neirynck also looks briefly at the arguments against the originality of Mark. First is source-critical methodology:

> Scholars have offered general criteria for deciding which is the more ancient among parallel traditions. [Edward] Sanders has examined these criteria: increasing length and detail, diminishing Semitism, and the use of direct discourse and conflation, as they occur both in the synoptic Gospels and in post-canonical material. His conclusion is that "the tradition developed in opposite directions" and therefore "dogmatic statements" on the basis of these criteria are never justified.

William R. Farmer has argued, notes Neirynck, against the criterion of increasing specificity; he proposed a new criterion, Palestinian or Jewish provenance, but this could be nothing more than re-Judaization. Sanders's message "can be understood as a warning against generalization rather than an invitation to synoptic skepticism. More important than his negative conclusion is the recommendation to be alert to 'the editorial tendencies of each particular writer.'"

Neirynck mentions B. H. Streeter's five arguments for the priority of Mark. The fourth of these is the primitive character of Mark as shown by that Gospel's use of phrases likely to cause offense—phrases omitted or toned down in the other Gospels—and a roughness of style and grammar, including the preservation of Aramaic words. "More simply we can distinguish two dimensions in a single argument for Markan priority: *taxis* or order . . . and *lexis* or style."

Then comes the awkward part for the Markan hypothesis, the Minor Agreements. These are passages, all of them short (some only a word or two), in which Matthew and Luke agree as against Mark. Often the passages are renderings peculiar enough that one would think two writers would not both stumble on them. If Matthew and Luke both depend on Mark in the Triple Tradition [where all three record an event in like language], then how can they agree with each other here and differ from Mark? Neirynck lists four possible answers:

1. Proto-Mark (or Urmarkus). Matthew and Luke used an earlier version of Mark, shorter than the canonical Mark (which accounts for negative agreements or common omissions) and different in wording (which accounts for coincidences in content, vocabulary, style, grammar).

2. Deutero-Mark. The Markan text which was used by Matthew and Luke differed slightly from our Mark because of textual corruption, revision, or edition.

3. Common source. Matthew and Luke depend on a source other than Mark, perhaps a primitive Gospel or oral tradition.

4. Luke's dependence on Matthew. Luke, who follows Mark as his basic source in the Triple Tradition, was acquainted with and influenced by Matthew.

Neirynck weighs the Minor Agreements differently than do other writers: "Although they are cited as objection number one against the priority of Mark, it can be argued that often these agreements are in fact not so striking and that for most of the 'significant' agreements a satisfactory redactional explanation can be given."

The concluding portion of his study considers alternative solutions to the synoptic problem, including a modified two-source theory (which balloons, in the case of M. E. Boismard, into four original sources, three intermediate Gospels, and the final canonical Gospels, with lines of connection between most of these) and the theory of Luke's dependence on Matthew, which produces three quite distinct sequences from B. C. Butler's (Matthew-Mark-Luke), to Austin Farrer's (Mark-Matthew-Luke), and to William R. Farmer and Bernard Orchard's (Matthew-Luke-Mark). Neirynck says,

In all three hypotheses, Luke borrowed the Double-Tradition material [that is, what Matthew and Luke have in common but Mark omits] from Matthew, and there is no need for a hypothetical say-ings source [that is, for Q]. With regard to Mark, conflicting views are defended: absolute priority of Mark (Farrer), Mark's depen-dence on Matthew (Butler), Mark as a secondary combination of Matthew and Luke (Farmer).

Until the eighteenth century, nearly everyone, whether amateur or scholar, presumed the Gospels were written in the order found in the New Testament. Then, two centuries ago, the synoptic fact became the synoptic problem. From the time of the Fathers it had been clear that the first three Evangelists used many of the same words and composed their Gospels in much the same sequence —but not entirely the same words and not entirely the same se-quence. This was not seen as warranting much investigation until the eighteenth century, when suddenly it became a concern, and the nineteenth century, when the concern turned into a problem.

By 1794 Johann Gottfried Eichhorn already had posed his fa-mous alternative: "Either the three [synoptic] Gospel writers made use of one another, or they depended upon a common source." The race was on, and so far the clear winners have been exponents of the theory of Markan priority, which holds not only that the Gospel of Mark was the first to be written but that it was to a large extent the origin of Matthew and Luke. Supplanted was the tradi-tional theory, known as the Augustinian, which held that Matthew wrote first, followed by Mark as a conflator of Matthew, and that Luke wrote last. The rise of critical biblical scholarship, which may be said to have begun in Eichhorn's era, coincided with the demise of what had been until then the almost-unanimous opinion of the few people who bothered to write about what later would be called the synoptic problem.

Here should be mentioned a position that has been revived in recent years and that seems to be gaining adherents: the Griesbach hypothesis. Johann Jacob Griesbach (1745–1812) summarized his position this way: "When Mark wrote his book he had in front of his eyes not only Matthew, but Luke as well, and he excerpted from them whatever he intended to preserve of the deeds, words, and destiny of the Savior." The Griesbach hypothesis achieved a certain celebrity in the early nineteenth century, and then it fell out of style as the Markan hypothesis took hold. In recent years —say, from the publication of William R. Farmer's *The Synoptic Problem* in 1964—it has made something of a comeback, but the main hypothesis, still, is the Markan.

The history of the Markan hypothesis consists of a series of forward steps combined with some backtracking. The way was led by Christian Gottlob Wilke, who published in 1838 a work titled *The Ur-Evangelist*. Wilke criticized earlier writers, including Eichhorn, who had posited vaguely some sort of ur-Gospel from which the canonical Gospels could have been drawn. The entire absence from history of any mention of such a work was, naturally enough, a substantial drawback to such a theory. Wilke found a way around it. The ur-Gospel, he said, has been before our eyes all the time—it is Mark itself! "It would be hard to exaggerate the surprise of his contemporaries," writes Hans-Herbert Stoldt. "This was a genuine academic sensation. No one before had given a thought to the possibility that the sought-after ur-Gospel, the foundation of the canonical Gospels, was in fact one of the latter."

Wilke's thesis was not without problems. It was based on his notion that "Mark is always the one accompanied"—that is, a comparison of parallel passages demonstrates that Matthew or Luke copied Mark, as proved by the commonality of the language. Of course, this begged the question, since a critic could (and critics did) say that perhaps it was Mark who did the following, copying Matthew here and Luke there. Working with the three Gospels alone, Wilke was unable to sustain his position. To the rescue came Christian Hermann Weisse, who posited a "sayings" collection. He identified this collection as the *logia* mentioned by Papias, who is quoted in Eusebius's *Ecclesiastical History*: "So then Matthew composed *ta logia* in the Hebrew language." This seemed to solve the difficulties apparent with using Mark as the sole source of Matthew and Luke. Weisse thought Papias must have been referring to a collection of Christ's sayings and teachings, something along the line of an ancient Bartlett's confined to quotations from one man.

Further reflection brought up a substantial difficulty: How to account for the common non-sayings material? If the sayings collection included all such matter, what one ended up with was, basically, Mark, which returned one to Wilke's position. If the sayings collection did not include material other than dominical sayings, then one could not account for common narrative portions. Heinrich Julius Holtzmann attempted to resolve such concerns. It is he who is commonly thought to have brought the Markan hypothesis to a state of completion in the form of the two-source theory. He did this in 1863. He postulated a historical source consisting of almost all of the canonical Mark, the short form of the Sermon on the Mount (Luke 6:20–49), and a few stray verses from John and Matthew, and he accepted a sayings collection or *logia*. According to Holtzmann, all three synoptics used these sources and therefore constitute variations of them, either by omission or addition. Mark, the shortest of the Gospels, contains little "historical" material. If some event did not appear in a particular Gospel, it is because it was omitted when a particular Evangelist copied from the historical source. Similarly for sayings: If a saying is missing from a Gospel, it is because the writer failed to copy it from the sayings source.

The weakness in Holtzmann's theory was that it could not answer why a particular writer would leave out a particular passage. Holtzmann argued it was an "unimportant" passage, so Matthew, say, left it out. Then why did not Mark also leave it out? Mark "left out" the Sermon on the Mount, but he "included" a parable chapter (Mark 4:1–34) which is five verses longer than Luke's version of the Sermon on the Mount. He also included an apocalypse (Mark 13:5–37), which is three verses longer. Why leave out one and keep the others? Are we to imagine Mark thought the Sermon on the Mount "unimportant"? Are the other passages "important" by comparison? Holtzmann's alternative notion that the Sermon on the Mount was dropped to save time prompts the question, "Why not save more time and drop the other passages also?"

William R. Farmer has written that Holtzmann's "most weighty point . . . was the scientifically gratuitous but powerfully apologetic fact that it was conceded by all contemporary critics that Matthew was secondary to the eye-witness period. This meant that the Griesbach hypothesis, as well as the Augustinian and all others which made Matthew the earliest of the Gospels, simply could not provide a viable solution to the source problem." The importance of this point is not to be minimized—Markan priority requires a late-written Matthew.

Paul Wernle is credited with developing, in 1899, an idea that since has been taken as self-evident by many scholars: The emergence of a longer work from a shorter is more easily explained than the emergence of a shorter work from a longer—enlargement is more likely to occur than abridgment. He continued this idea by saying a longer work may be not just an expansion of a shorter but a combination of a shorter with outside sources. These sources themselves might form a series, one dependent on the other. Applied to the Gospels, Wernle called these multiple sources "Q" (he identified seven Q sources in all). Unlike the *logia* mentioned by Papias, Q, in its various forms, was not confined to sayings material but included narrative material (thus *logia* would not be a proper term for it).

The perfection of the two-source theory came with Bernhard Weiss (1827–1918), professor of New Testament at the University of Berlin. This "perfection" came not so much from a new insight—Weiss argued that Q could not be confined to sayings materials but also must include narrative material, but he was not the first to suggest this—as from Weiss's status as perhaps the top biblical scholar of his time. His approbation of the two-source theory gave it a momentum it might not otherwise have sustained.

The greatest drag on the theory all along had been the gratuitousness of Q: Aside from Papias's line about the *logia*, there was nothing at all to suggest that a document (or collection of documents) such as Q existed. No one mentioned it, and its disappearance from history seems remarkable. If the synoptics were all dependent on it, how could it have been allowed to disappear? If an epistle as inconsequential as Philemon had been preserved carefully for eighteen centuries, why had not Q, an immeasurably more important document?

Although the argument for Markan priority was developed first and almost exclusively by German scholars, in this century the argument has been carried in large part by English scholars, the chief among them being B. H. Streeter, who made five main points:

1. Matthew reproduces ninety percent of Mark, and Luke reproduces more than half, in language nearly identical with that of Mark. This is the argument from content.

2. In passages found in all three synoptics, Matthew or Luke or both are in verbal agreement with Mark, and they almost never agree against Mark. This is the argument from wording.

3. The ordering of incidents seems more original in Mark and is, on the whole, supported by Matthew and Luke. When one of the latter departs from the Markan pattern, the other is found to support it. This is the argument from arrangement.

4. Mark's language is rough. Matthew and Luke improve it. This is the argument from language.

5. The way in which material—both Markan and non-Markan —is distributed throughout the other synoptics suggests each was working independently with Mark plus some other sources.

Streeter outlined these considerations in *The Four Gospels: A Study of Origins*. He rejected attempts to revive the Augustinian hypothesis:

The attempt has recently been made to revive the solution, first put forward by Augustine, who styles Mark a kind of abridger and lackey of Matthew . . . But Augustine did not possess a synopsis of the Greek text conveniently printed in parallel columns. Otherwise a person of his intelligence could not have failed to perceive that, where the two Gospels are parallel, it is usually Matthew, and not Mark, who does the abbreviation. For example, the number of words employed by Mark to tell the stories of the Gadarene demoniac, Jairus's daughter, and the feeding of the five thousand are respectively 325, 374, and 235; Matthew contrives to tell them in 136, 135, and 157 words. Now there is nothing antecedently improbable in the idea that for certain purposes an abbreviated version of the Gospel might be desired, but only a lunatic would leave out

Matthew's account of the infancy, the Sermon on the Mount, and practically all the parables, in order to get room for purely verbal expansion of what was retained.

Streeter's confident style naturally enough attracted followers and expanders, one of the most prominent of whom has been Joseph A. Fitzmyer, who terms Streeter's fifth argument his weakest and who explains that the priority of Mark can be found in the more primitive character of the narrative, what might be termed its freshness and circumstantial character. Mark's phrases are more likely to cause offense, his grammar and style are rough, and he preserves Aramaic words.

Today the hypothesis of Markan priority relies on half a dozen main proofs; they are basically duplicative of the proofs given by Streeter. Each has undergone development, each has its partisans and critics. The basic proof is what Karl Lachmann, in 1835, called the "proof from order." Weisse had put it this way: "It is precisely this consideration which carries the ultimate, decisive weight in favor of our view on the mutual relationship of the synoptic Gospels." William Wrede, writing in 1901, said that "the strength of the Markan hypothesis lies specifically in the fact that the sequence of the narratives in Mark underlies the sequence in Matthew and Luke." This is a key point, but not one accepted by all. Some ask whether there is really a common sequence, a common narrative thread that can be isolated and agreed upon by scholars, or is the truth what Stoldt, a chief critic of the two-source hypothesis, claims, "that there is neither a continuous actual nor even a merely reconstructible common narrative line. . . . There are only shifting parallels between Mark on the one hand and Matthew and Luke on the other, sometimes with one, sometimes with the other"? The proof from order depends on, in Weisse's words, the concurrence of the three synoptics being "always mediated by Mark."

Stoldt argues that

Weisse makes a serious error in logic. For if all three synoptic authors concur with one another, it does not necessarily follow that

the concurrence of the other two is "always mediated by Mark."
This is readily shown by the simple fact that one could just as well
reverse the conclusion: Mark concurs with Matthew and Luke only
as long as these two agree with each other, but, whenever they do not
agree with each other, Mark concurs with neither. Consequently,
the concurrence of Mark with these two is always mediated solely
by the agreement of these two with each other.

This problem was recognized by B. C. Butler, who reproduces
an example taken from E. A. Abbott's *The Fourfold Gospel*:

> Matthew and Luke are in the position of two schoolboys, Primus
> and Tertius, seated on the same form, between whom sits another,
> Secundus (Mark). All three are writing (we will suppose) a narra-
> tive of the same event. . . . Primus and Tertius copy largely from
> Secundus. Occasionally the two copy the same words; then we have
> agreement of the three writers. At other times Primus (Matthew)
> copies what Tertius (Luke) does not. . . . But Primus and Tertius
> cannot look over each other's shoulders, and hence agreement of
> them "against" Secundus is only an accident. As the same results
> (exactly) will follow, if Secundus copied from Primus (or Tertius)
> and was himself copied by Tertius (or Primus), we must hope that
> Abbott, who was headmaster of a famous school, was not illustrat-
> ing from real life.

The second main proof of Markan priority is the proof from
uniformity. It is based on the proof from order. Mark's is the only
Gospel that exhibits an unbroken narrative continuity. It forms a
whole. By comparison, the other synoptics seem to lack continuity. Stoldt says,

> When one juxtaposes the other two synoptic Gospels against Mark,
> they could scarcely be more different. Compared to Mark they ap-
> pear to lack unity; one can even say that they are poorly composed.
> A major block of discourse is inserted into the middle of Matthew's
> historical narrative. In Luke the genealogy is interpolated inorgan-
> ically between the baptism and the temptation, interrupting the
> previous train of thought.

The proof from originality is repeated by nearly every advo-
cate of Markan priority. Mark gives the impression of having been

composed on its own, at once, by one man; it does not seem to be a revision of another's work, nor does it seem to be composed of sections so disparate in style that a reader would suspect them to have been lifted from earlier writings.

The proof from language is thought by some scholars to be the weakest of the several proofs since it is rather subjective. Mark's writing is said to be the most immature, and this suggests it came first. Matthew and Luke are more polished, suggesting they came later or at least suggesting that they may have borrowed from Mark but that Mark probably would not have borrowed from them (and then introduced rougher language).

The proof from doublets has been one of the main supports of the theory of Markan priority, a doublet occurring when a variant reading of an incident is given. Matthew and Luke share five doublets; Matthew has six others proper to his Gospel, and Luke has three others proper to his. A doublet may arise when an author finds two sources describing what is apparently the same event in slightly different ways. He incorporates both descriptions into his new work. The argument from doublets has been criticized on the grounds that Mark also contains doublets, implying that the argument as a whole proves nothing either way.

The last of the major proofs is the one from the Petrine origin of Mark. If Mark had been a close follower of Peter's, and if he wrote down Peter's remarks about the Lord, as reported by Papias, then one could argue toward a relatively early date for Mark—at least relative to the other synoptics. Curiously, Stoldt takes considerable pains to counter this argument, even though it is not the key argument for Markan priority, yet he does so unconvincingly. If Mark really were Peter's follower, he says, then "one would have every right to expect that the figure of Peter would not only take a central position in the Gospel of Mark but also, beyond that, would stand out considerably more than in the other Gospels. This, however, is not the case—on the contrary." It is curious that Stoldt should say this since many writers have argued precisely the opposite from Peter's lack of prominence in Mark. It has been said that if Mark had been Peter's disciple, it is likely he knew a Peter who was self-effacing, quick to recount his own failings (such as the triple denial), and reluctant to recount anything that might be to his credit. A faithful disciple of such a teacher would tend to follow his teacher's example (and wishes?) and minimize Peter's role. In other words, Mark's relative silence concerning Peter argues in favor of, not against, Mark's having been in Peter's company.

The chief critic of the Markan hypothesis in the English-speaking world has been William R. Farmer. He has been at the center of an increasingly influential, but still minority, school of thought. This school has been promoted through seminars, festivals, colloquia, and conferences, beginning around 1966, and in a series of works, many published by Mercer University Press. In *The Synoptic Problem* Farmer gave new credence to the Griesbach hypothesis and criticized the received position of Markan priority. This is not to say he was the first to find fault with the majority position. "In 1951, B. C. Butler called attention to the fallacy of the argument from order when taken on Streeter's terms, and Butler's analysis of the fallaciousness of Streeter's reasoning at this point was cogently reiterated at Cambridge by G. M. Styler."

Farmer summarized the development of the two-source hypothesis, looking at the period up to and culminating in Holtzmann, then focusing on the English endorsement of the German position. After an extended critique of Streeter's arguments, Farmer looked at the intellectual climate which, he said, allowed the Markan hypothesis to reign unchallenged for so many decades. He identified a kind of silent argument:

> Eventually a new argument was to develop which, though it never appeared in print, exercised a greater influence in sustaining belief in the priority of Mark than any that Streeter or anyone else has ever published. This argument may be formally stated as follows: "It is inconceivable that so many scholars could have been so wrong on such a fundamental point for such a long period of time." This is a powerful argument precisely because in practice it is irrefutable. Every scholar respects honest humility and sincere pietas in his colleague. The critic who sets his judgment against a consensus endorsed by the vast majority of experts during a long period of

time does so at the risk of being guilty of academic arrogance and of losing the confidence of his colleagues.

Farmer has not been the only well-known scholar writing against Markan priority. On the Catholic side (Farmer joined the Catholic Church a few years ago, but his important early writings were written while he was a Methodist) there has been Bernard Orchard, O.S.B., a Benedictine monk of Ealing Abbey in London. In 1976 he published *Matthew, Luke & Mark*, which was his first extended treatment of the problem. In that work he described himself as

> following up the work begun over forty years ago by Dom John Chapman and continued by Bishop B. C. Butler and then by Professor William R. Farmer. . . . For them, and for me too, the two-document hypothesis and the priority of Mark are still only hypotheses, not infallible dogmas, and they have stood secure for so long chiefly because no one has been able to offer any satisfactory alternative.

Orchard tried to sketch such an alternative. He hoped to follow up quickly with two further volumes, but his plans changed, and eleven years later, with Harold Riley, an Anglican priest and later a convert, he published *The Order of the Synoptics: Why Three Synoptic Gospels?*

Unlike most other commentators, Orchard and Riley did not feel compelled to confine themselves to literary or internal arguments. Such evidence is examined by Riley in the first section of the book. Then Orchard tackles the historical tradition, looking at the works of early Christian writers and heretics, both before and after Papias. Finally there comes a synthesis of the internal and external evidence, the authors concluding that Matthew was written between 30 and 44 and that if a date after 70 is posited, "then the problem of its relationships to the other Gospels becomes insoluble." They see the Gospels as having been "the reactions of the Church's leaders to the successive phases through which the pre-70 Church is known to have passed—crises which can actually be pinpointed."

John A. T. Robinson, an Anglican bishop, said he wanted to take a fresh look at the presuppositions used in dating the New Testament books, presuppositions which, he thought, had not been reexamined critically since the nineteenth century. This look convinced him the presuppositions were little more than prejudices. He started from scratch and concluded that every book of the New Testament was written prior to the fall of Jerusalem in 70. The Gospels of Matthew, Luke, and even John he put as early as the forties. Robinson "worked from an exclusively historical methodology," wrote Jean Carmignac in *The Birth of the Synoptics*. Carmignac, a Dead Sea Scrolls translator and an expert in the Hebrew in use at the time of Christ, reached conclusions similar to Robinson's, but he came at the problem from a different angle. He translated the synoptic Gospels "backwards," from Greek into Hebrew, and was astonished at what he found.

"I wanted to begin with the Gospel of Mark," he said,

[i]n order to facilitate the comparison between our Greek Gospels and the Hebrew text of Qumran, I tried, for my own personal use, to see what Mark would yield when translated back into the Hebrew of Qumran. I had imagined that this translation would be difficult because of considerable differences between Semitic thought and Greek thought, but I was absolutely dumbfounded to discover that this translation was, on the contrary, extremely easy. Around the middle of April 1963, after only one day of work, I was convinced that the Greek text of Mark could not have been redacted directly in Greek and that it was in reality only the Greek translation of an original Hebrew.

Carmignac had planned for enormous difficulties, but they did not arise. He discovered the Greek translator of Mark had slavishly kept to the Hebrew word order and grammar. Could this have been the result of a Semite writing in Greek, a language he didn't know too well and on which he imposed Hebrew structures? Or could the awkward phrasings found in our Greek text have been nothing more than overly faithful translations (perhaps "transliterations" would be more accurate) of Semitic originals? If the second possibility were true, then we have synoptic Gospels written by eyewitnesses at a very early date.

Carmignac spent most of the next twenty-five years meticulously translating the Greek into Hebrew and making endless comparisons. *The Birth of the Synoptics* is a popular summary of what he hoped to publish in a massive multi-volume set. Some consider it a disturbing book—which it is. Let's consider just one example of what he discovered.

The Benedictus, the song of Zachary, is given in Luke 1:68–79. In Greek, as in English, the Benedictus seems unexceptional as poetry. There is no evidence of clever composition. But, when it is translated into Hebrew, a little marvel appears. In the phrase "to show mercy to our fathers," the expression "to show mercy" is the Hebrew verb *hânan*, which is the root of the name *Yôhânân* (John). In "he remembers his holy covenant," "he remembers" is the verb *zâkar*, which is the root of the name *Zâkâryâh* (Zachary). In "the oath which he swore to our father Abraham" is found, for "to take an oath," the verb *shâba*, which is the root of the name Elîshâba (Elizabeth).

Carmignac asks, "Is it by chance that the second strophe of this poem begins by a triple allusion to the names of the three protagonists: John, Zachary, Elizabeth? But this allusion exists only in Hebrew; the Greek or English translation does not preserve it." He explains that

> Hebrew has a great preference for plays on words, and it takes great pleasure in making reference to similar sounds, which facilitate the task of memorization. Another typical case is hidden in the Our Father (Matt. 6:12–13), in which the word "forgive" corresponds to the root *nâsâ*, "debts and debtors" to *nâshâh*, and "temptation" to *nasah*. Is this yet another case of mere chance? Isn't it reasonable to think that these words have been chosen by design in order to produce a sort of internal rhyme?

Carmignac gives many other examples, and he draws these conclusions about the dating of the synoptics: "The latest dates that can be admitted are around 50 for Mark . . . around 55 for Completed Mark, around 55–60 for Matthew, between 58 and 60 for Luke. But the earliest dates are clearly more probable: Mark around 42, Completed Mark around 45, (Hebrew) Matthew around 50, (Greek) Luke a little after 50." These dates are all approximate, of course, particularly those for Mark and Matthew, and they are the result of Carmignac's mainly philological analysis. Carmignac draws a few other conclusions:

> 1. It is certain that Mark, Matthew, and the documents used by Luke were redacted in a Semitic language.
> 2. It is probable that this Semitic language is Hebrew rather than Aramaic.
> 3. It is sufficiently probable that our second Gospel [that is, Mark] was composed in a Semitic language by St. Peter the Apostle (with Mark being his secretary perhaps).

Expanding on this last point, he says that "it is probable that the Semitic Gospel of Peter was translated into Greek, perhaps with some adaptations by Mark, in Rome, at the latest around the year 63; it is our second Gospel which has preserved the name of the translator, instead of that of the author."

As he wrote, Carmignac suspected his "scientific arguments [would] prove reassuring to Christians and [would] attract the attention and interest of non-believers. But they overturn theories presently in vogue and therefore they will be fiercely criticized." They may also be, with Carmignac's death, fiercely (and quite unjustly) ignored.

Claude Tresmontant, a member of the faculty at the Sorbonne, wrote *The Hebrew Christ*, in which he takes, like Robinson, something of a historical approach, but also, like Carmignac, something of a philological approach. He combines the two and comes up with a provocative thesis: All four Gospels were written in Hebrew first, then translated. Hebrew Matthew was written shortly after the Resurrection, followed within a few years by a Greek translation. Hebrew John was written by 36, then also quickly translated. Luke came next, being written between 40 and 60, and Mark probably came last, being written between 50 and 60, but Mark may have squeaked in front of Luke.

Tresmontant sets aside what he regards as unwarranted historical presuppositions and tries to examine each Gospel cold, as it were. Throughout his book he notes the Evangelists' references to persecution. Who were the persecutors? He suggests they probably were not Romans working under Nero's orders after 64, since the New Testament almost never warns against Romans. The warnings are almost always couched in terms of the Jewish authorities, and anti-Christian sentiment was evident early on—witness the stoning of Stephen. It's more likely, then, that the persecutions that form the backdrop to many passages in the New Testament occurred not late in the first century but by the middle of it. Tresmontant, writing of Matthew, says:

> It does not date only from the end of the first century A.D., as the majority of exegetes hold today. All the indications, signs, and characteristics of the book we call the Gospel according to Matthew point to a very ancient period, a period only shortly after the momentous events of A.D. 30—certainly before the first joyous proclamation of the good news of Christ to the pagans and the uncircumcised which occurred around A.D. 36–40. There is absolutely nothing in this Gospel that would lead us to suppose that it was composed later; there is no text, nor any fragment of a text; there is not so much as a mark; there is nothing. The claim that the Gospel according to Matthew was only composed toward the end of the first century is a totally arbitrary claim. The only thing this claim has going for it is that fact that the majority opinion among exegetes today supports it. That is simply to say that the opinion rests upon nothing but itself.

Making a pericope-by-pericope examination of much of Matthew, Tresmontant points to the exclusively Jewish provenance of the writing. This is not just a matter of style. It is also a matter of substance. Matthew writes for an audience composed of Jews, not Greeks. But the Church quickly ceased to be a solely Jewish affair, which implies a very early dating for Matthew. Similarly the other Gospels are given early dates.

Along the way Tresmontant junks opinions that have been taken as a matter of course by many scholars. Luke's Gospel, for instance, is often said to be the one with the best Greek. But Tresmontant says that, "contrary to the general belief that has served as the conventional wisdom for some time, the Gospel according to Luke is the least Greek of the four and the most Hebrew (except for its first phrase)." He argues that

> it is probably because of these first four verses that scholars for a long time have praised the literary style of Luke and have considered Luke an especially well educated writer, a Hellenist, and the like. From verse 5 on, however—and practically to the end of this Gospel —the Greek style of Luke is no longer quite so natural. Rather, it is manifestly a Greek that has been translated, and translated from the Hebrew at that!

As for Mark, Tresmontant says,

> I do not hold with the majority opinion of scholars regarding the composition of Mark. I do not believe that Mark was the first Gospel written. I certainly do not think that it is older than Matthew. On the contrary, all the indications point to a very ancient date for the composition of Matthew. Not all of these same indications apply in the case of Mark. We need only think, for example, of the sayings of our Lord in which he indicated that he was sent to preach exclusively to the Hebrew people, to save only the lost sheep of Israel. The sayings concerning the sign of Jonah are similarly not to be found in Mark. Also, the text of Mark tends to eliminate some of the words or phrases which would have grated most harshly on the ear of the educated Greek.

This is the way in which Tresmontant summarizes his position:

> In asserting that documents written in Hebrew lie behind the present Greek text of our four Gospels, we are, of course, proceeding by way of a hypothesis. Here, however, we are dealing with a hypothesis that has to be true—indeed, has to be considered certain— because it is the only hypothesis capable of explaining all the features that we find in the Greek text of the Gospels. The contrary hypothesis is that a long tradition of oral preaching and transmission preceded the setting down in writing at a comparatively late date of the Greek text of the four Gospels as we presently possess it. The contrary position is the one preferred by the majority of biblical scholars today, as has been the case for more than a century.

In the epilogue, Tresmontant says that, as he

> became more familiar with the subject matter, I began to perceive
> difficulties. Then I encountered some simple impossibilities. Fi-
> nally, the entire superstructure collapsed like the proverbial house
> of cards. The more I studied the Old Testament the more I began
> to recognize the Hebraic phraseology behind the Greek in each of
> the four Gospels. Eventually, I arrived at the conclusions that I have
> tried to set forth in this book: Matthew and John wrote the earliest
> Gospels; those of Luke and Mark were written later; all four of
> the Gospels, as well as some of the other New Testament books,
> were evidently translations into Greek from earlier texts originally
> composed in Hebrew.

Tresmontant notes that

> philosophical assumptions, like philosophical preferences and dis-
> likes, have always played a considerable role in the great scientific
> debates and controversies of the past. In the history of biblical schol-
> arship and exegesis, it is evident that such philosophical assump-
> tions adopted prior to any objective exegesis have played an equally
> considerable role. Ernest Renan openly declared this to be the case
> in the famous preface to the thirteenth edition of his *Life of Jesus*.

Tresmontant's theory is too new to have been subjected yet to
the critical examination required of any theory. In a way he uses
John A. T. Robinson's method of attack: Set aside presuppositions
and examine the text raw—then explain what you see. His familiarity with the Hebrew of the Dead Sea Scrolls and his willing-
ness to step on scholarly toes makes his a provocative thesis. If he
is correct that the Gospels were Hebrew compositions first and
that they therefore must have been written early, and if Matthew
is more ancient in style than Mark, then not only has Markan
priority been disproved, but so has the existence of Q, which,
generally, has been posited as necessary if the Gospels were written fairly late in the first century. If they were written within a
decade or two of the events they report (or even within a handful
of years, in the case of Matthew), Q is superfluous.

Jean Carmignac and Claude Tresmontant worked parallel to one another, not in concert, not in tandem. Their conclusions are similar but distinct. Both hold to Hebrew originals, not just Hebrew scraps included among the (mainly Greek) documents used by the authors. Both hold to early datings. But Carmignac came down in favor of Markan priority (though not insisting on it), while Tresmontant insisted the first Gospel to be written was Matthew's.

It is too early to say what response will be given to these French scholars. Carmignac and Tresmontant are dead, and the dead can be ignored easily. Tresmontant, moreover, wrote with only a minimum of diplomacy and nuance; he may not be taken seriously, even if his ideas should be. However that may be, their books are signs the discussion remains open and lively. Indeed, "in recent years the discussion of the synoptic problem has been much more lively than it has been for a generation," wrote Lamar Cope.

> Most sensitive critics are aware that many of the arguments which led to the consensus that Mark is the earliest Gospel and that there was a source Q are, in themselves, circular or fallacious. . . . [Nevertheless], the great majority of New Testament critics trained in the milieu of the scholarship of the last half century will still retain the workability of the Mark-Q hypothesis in some general form as the best available solution to the problem of the relationships among the Gospels. . . . But whatever the critical and historical consequences may be, new evidence about the structure of the key passages points unmistakably toward the literary priority of the Gospel of Matthew over Mark and Luke. Unless this evidence is countered successfully, nothing—scholarly consensus, scholarly reputation, or vehement denial—can rescue the priority of Mark.

If the last twenty years saw a discussion "more lively than it has been for a generation," the next twenty may see one livelier still. The scholars following Farmer will continue to undermine Markan priority. Those following Carmignac and Tresmontant will undermine late dating. Those adhering to what is now the majority opinion will attempt to shore up their positions. It may be that what has been regarded as an "assured result of modern biblical scholarship" will be regarded as anything but assured, or it may be that the upstart theories, by calling attention to themselves, will have invited precisely the scrutiny that will insure their downfall.

9

I Think Therefore I Am (I Think)

Only an old prospector's face could be more wrinkled than Fred's shirt. The tiny creases are so crisp they must have been made with a midget's iron. The faded blue of his shirt heightens his natural pallor, and his quick tongue and Buckleyesque grin mark him as one of those lean and hungry men who think too much. Caesar would not have approved. But the dozen people gathered for the weekly meeting of the Philosopher's Forum seem content. Most are apparently regulars, but there are a few faces, mine included, that betray their wearers as strangers. There might be more strangers present, I say to myself, were it not for the group's name.

When I was in high school, a friend asked if I wanted to take the entrance examination for Mensa, the smart people's club. I put him off, and perhaps he thought I was afraid of not passing. What really stopped me was that there was no way to try out for Mensa without looking conceited. By taking its test you affirm that you think you are among the intellectual elite. I suspect the same disability plagues the Philosopher's Forum. Its title is a presumption, and even the name of the newsletter claims too much; it is called "Free Wisdom." A little more humility, I think as I gaze around the room, might attract a lot more people.

Meetings are held Wednesday nights in a dark and worn house in an older section of town. The front room is large and unheated, and the outside's coolness seems intensified. The wooden floor is partly covered by mismatched throw rugs, and on the walls are frayed tapestries that no doubt were willed by some old maiden aunt whose aesthetic taste never caught up with her years.

Fred is hugged by a chair that has lost its stuffing. He is thin and obviously well-read, at least in a certain limited area of philosophy and politics. He styles himself a jack of several trades, and in the near past he has been a disc jockey, part owner of a dating service, and, most recently, an employee of a photocopying shop. On the sofa near Fred sits Jack. He delights in taking pot shots at well-known figures and in sparring with Fred, who takes a decidedly libertarian approach to economics. Jack is an unreconstructed socialist who claims that "this city is culturally sterile." He proposes to do something about it, but he gives no specifics.

In the corner nearest and slightly behind me sits a young man who says nothing all evening. He smiles at particularly nasty cracks, and it is said that he considers himself a hedonist. He does not look the part. A hedonist, as we all know, should look like a fading Italian movie star whose hirsute and once manly chest has become an extension of his waistline. Sporting two days' stubble and clothes that rival Fred's in disarray, this fellow does not seem the sort who preens himself at length each morning.

My consideration of the people in the room is broken by Jack's remarks about Mensa. "The people in Mensa have high IQs but low intelligence." No one disagrees, and one suspects there may be several cases of sour grapes. Yet Jack may have a point. Mensa's level of discourse is no doubt lower than strangers might think and members might say. The same, perhaps, can be said about the Philosopher's Forum, and in retrospect it is clear that this group is best thought of as a continuation of college bull sessions.

"How should we go about solving major social problems?" someone asks. The silence broken, there follows general chatter (except from the guy in the corner), and it is concluded by the most vociferous that utilitarianism will provide the best answers. There is general agreement that no one present knows how to manipulate the utilitarian balance, which makes the discussion appear a little futile. How much does freedom weigh against security? Truth against beauty? Which is more important, happiness or peace? Are all these categories distinct, and are they categories at all, and have we come up with a type of Platonism in spite of ourselves?

The topics shift. Someone brings up Epicureanism, but his voice is lost in arguments about situation ethics. Then the conversation turns to education. Should it be provided by the state or by private institutions only? Fred condemns the state, and that gleam in his eye shows that he has read too much Ayn Rand. "Nonsense," intones Jack, quick with the socialist reply. "With private schools only, you would have chaos, lack of standards, and, worst, monopolies."

"What do you think we have now with compulsory public education?" retorts a woman who has been sitting on the floor and fiddling with the heel to her shoe. She says nothing more the rest of the night.

Margaret Mead's name comes up several times, flashing across the room like a benediction, and several comments are made on the sense or nonsense of cultural relativism. At this point another woman asks if we are determined in our actions by the environment or by genetic factors. (No one asks: Are we determined at all?) She receives no answer.

"The survival instinct is the basis of all ethics," pipes up a man who takes the contrary position on most issues, even to the point of contradicting what he said earlier. For twenty minutes, the group considers his statement and concludes it has merit, but not much. The logic begins to show signs of strain. Syllogisms fly back and forth the way jugglers pass bowling pins to one another, yet the final conclusions seem perverse. No one is quite satisfied.

I am reminded of a professor at one of the local law schools, a young man full of promise, who wrote an essay on the ethics of abortion. His syllogisms led him to the conclusion that not only must abortion be permitted but that infanticide and the killing of children under the age of reason should be legalized. "I don't know what to do or where my thinking went wrong," he admitted to me. "I have a great revulsion for infanticide and the killing of children, of course, and even for abortion. My emotions tell me they are morally wrong, but my logic forces me to accept them." His logic brought him into a Kafkaesque world.

That world could be found again in this front room. Probabilities are piled on top of each other to a dizzying height, resulting in improbabilities with the force of mental law. As the evening wears on, the dissatisfaction becomes palpable, even as the camaraderie grows. Perhaps reason has distinct limits, particularly for amateurs.

During the long evening there is no universal agreement on any point, save, perhaps, for a permeating anti-theistic bias that makes me feel the outsider. This bias is not surprising. The leaders of the Philosopher's Forum, Fred and Jack, are longtime members of the Humanist Association and are officers of that group. The Humanists oppose religion the way policemen oppose crooks, and perhaps it is not wrong to say they daily relive the Scopes "monkey trial" of 1925, the case pitting Clarence Darrow against William Jennings Bryan on the issue of teaching evolutionism rather than creationism in the schools.

A recent newsletter from the Humanist Association went to members and guests of the Philosopher's Forum. It included a survey designed to find out what the Association's members wanted their organization to do. The primary statement was, "I want the main thrust of the Humanist Association to be," and possible answers were: "(a) Against the churches and organized religion," "(b) Against theology and religious beliefs," and "(c) Against rising cults and Far-Eastern religious sects." There was an option, later on, of "(j) Other." I presume this would include the contrary of what was earlier listed, and here a member could write in projects in favor of churches, organized religion, theology, religious beliefs, rising cults, Far-Eastern sects, and other things Humanists point their lances at. At the bottom of the newsletter, the survey ended with the dreary statistic that nine out of ten Americans believe in God, which shows just how far the Humanists have to go.

The meeting of the Philosopher's Forum inches past midnight and is winding up. Next week, and for most following weeks, there will be a topic assigned in advance. But the group's leaders dream if they think these people will follow any agenda. Too many uncontained thoughts keep rising to the surface, and there is not enough discipline to keep them within.

"I hope you come back next week," Fred says to the new faces. He apparently hopes for people with a variety of views. "Tell your friends about our meetings. My number is in the book." We file out one by one, turning down the dark street and taking with us, perhaps, fond memories of late-night debates in college dormitories mixed with frustration regarding tonight's exchange. I wonder whether other participants suspect (and perhaps fear) that the evening's evident sterility points, ultimately, to the fecundity of the Catholic faith. I wonder who, in twenty years, will have found answers in the only place they are to be found and who will be trapped, as in amber, in discussions like this.

Ayn Rand vs. Catholicism

Because recent popes have defended private property and a regime of liberty, many Catholics look at least paternally on anyone who makes an attempt to promote or defend capitalism. There can be a danger in this, especially among younger, impressionable Catholics who might get carried away in their advocacy of the free market. In their zeal they may combine forces with people who have less than the good of the Church at heart. In a time when Christendom has all but vanished and been replaced by a purely secular culture, it is important for us to know with whom we Catholics can make alliances and with whom we must not.

One of those falling in the latter group is Ayn Rand (1905–1982), the popular novelist and campus cult figure. Known particularly for her avid defense of *laissez-faire* capitalism and a personal ideology she called Objectivism, Rand was less than friendly toward organized religion, and this applied most especially to the Catholic Church. Her ideas remain popular on campus and off, her books still sell in the hundreds of thousands each year, and in intellectual circles her views have achieved a modicum of respectability. Nowadays, when the government is taking ever more authority from individuals, many of her isolated writings—especially her major novels, which have a certain Nietzschean glory about them—pluck the right heartstrings. Even good Catholics are moved, and it is not uncommon to see members of Christ's Mystical Body abruptly turn, under Rand's tutelage, into opponents of "mysticism"—her name for religion.

In 1967 Ayn Rand published a series of essays under the title *Capitalism: The Unknown Ideal.* Her several contributions to this book included a defense of big business, but not of government intervention therein; a consideration of the history of American free enterprise; a look at the status of airwaves, patents, and copyrights; and a discussion of the roots of war. The most pertinent essay, to a Catholic, was one entitled "Requiem for Man." The topic: Pope Paul VI's encyclical *Populorum Progressio*. Rand's long analysis of this important document included this introductory remark: "The encyclical is the manifesto of an impassioned hatred for capitalism." This summed up her whole argument. This Vicar of Christ wrote an encyclical composed of "impassioned hatred"; more than that, this papal document was a "manifesto," a fighting platform. And Rand certainly was looking for a fight.

Her analysis began by quoting from the encyclical: "But it is unfortunate," said Pope Paul

> that on these new conditions [the Industrial Revolution] of society a system has been constructed which considers profit as the key motive for economic progress, competition as the supreme law of economics, and private ownership of the means of production as an absolute right that has no limits and carries no corresponding social obligation. . . . But if it is true that a type of capitalism has been the source of extensive suffering, injustices, and fratricidal conflicts whose effects still persist, it would also be wrong to attribute to industrialization itself evils that belong to the woeful system that accompanied it.

This was the first quotation on which Rand made an attack, but it was not an entire quotation. The ellipsis left out essential points that clarified the meaning, namely: "This unchecked liberalism leads to dictatorship rightly denounced by Pius XI as producing 'the international imperialism of money.' One cannot condemn such abuse too strongly by solemnly recalling once again that the economy is at the service of man." From her partial quotation Rand concluded that Pope Paul roundly condemned the whole free market and took us by the hand into the socialist camp. But let's take a more careful look, particularly at what she failed to quote. What the Pope condemned are absolutizations. When profit is the key motive and competition the supreme law, when they are above all else, charity can have no part in economics—nor can a consideration that the earth was created by God for man and that man is really in a caretaker role. An absolute right to property, as distinguished from the large but not absolute right defended by Leo XIII in *Rerum Novarum*, would lead to absurd consequences.

For example, Southern California gets almost all its water from the Colorado River or from aqueducts that move water from the northern end of the state to the southern. Assume that a certain individual owned a millimeterwide strip of land encircling Southern California. Any aqueduct bringing water to Los Angeles would have to cross the skinny strip. Further assume that the strip's owner one day refuses to allow the water to pass over his land. The result under Rand's absolute-right system? Millions of thirsty Angelenos. Under our current system of law, built on ancient British common law extending back to a time when even Britain was professedly Christian, a few yards of the tiny strip would be condemned under eminent domain, and the owner would be given the nickel the land would be worth. The aqueducts would be operational again. The difference? An allowance for charity and for other considerations that are higher in value than rights to physical property. The great sufferings that would ensue on a lack of a water supply would be declared easily to outweigh an individual's interest in a useless strip of land. Such are the dangers of absolutizing certain rights.

The papal phraseology that Rand neglected to reproduce is also important. Here the Holy Father talked about "unchecked liberalism," its true abuses, and the fact that the economy must be made to serve man so he may serve God. Couple this with the Pope's statement that he was talking about only a "type of capitalism," and one realizes that he was not condemning the economic system outright but only certain variants that exclude the application of Christian social principles. But Ayn Rand saw capitalism as a monolith, unchanging and uncompromising. Either we accept all of her kind of capitalism—a kind that leaves little room for Christian virtues and in fact flies in the face of some of them—or we reject the free market entirely and opt for some sort of economic night. Such were her alternatives.

Contrast this with what we find in *The Servile State*. In this

1912 book Hilaire Belloc said that the free market (he did not use that term—it came into vogue later—but the meaning is the same) could have produced the same kinds of things and in the same amounts but without the excesses and the sufferings. Capital could have been raised through guilds and cooperatives rather than through impersonal industries suffering from giantism. Since the same capital could have been available, the same production could have occurred. The control of production would have been diffused, personal, and responsible. In the modern corporation ownership is divorced from responsibility and personal stake through stocks and other such arrangements, and control is vested in offices to be filled, not in individuals. (In this sense large corporations are anti-individualistic in that they separate function from responsibility and so bifurcate the individual.)

Back to encyclicals. These papal documents are not designed to be capsule history lessons. There was no need for Pope Paul to go into any detail to explain what he meant by "extensive suffering, injustices, and fratricidal conflicts" caused by capitalism. These should be known to any student of history and to anyone who realizes that all economic systems are liable to such faults. The argument that under capitalism some kinds of evils have been lessened is no response to the truth that even one evil is too many. Cardinal Newman, in his *Apologia Pro Vita Sua*, has an eloquent paragraph in which he explains why it is better for the cosmos to collapse and all men to die miserably of starvation than to have one man commit one venial sin. In the face of God, all sins are too large. So, there is no good reason to overlook those sins that may have and still do accompany capitalism, and there is no sense in trying to wish away injustices merely because anti-capitalists exploit them for propaganda purposes.

Rand further faulted *Populorum Progressio* because it "does not discuss or condemn any social system other than capitalism." She said that "one must conclude that all other systems are compatible with the encyclical's political philosophy." Where does one begin with such thinking? Socialism was roundly condemned in Leo XIII's *Rerum Novarum*, communism in Pius XI's *Atheistic Commu-*

nism, and fascism in Pius XII's *Mit Brennender Sorge*. There was no need to regurgitate these. Encyclicals must be understood in the light of one another, as parts of the whole corpus of papal teaching. It does not follow, as Rand insisted, that "one must conclude" that all other systems aside from capitalism are compatible with Catholicism. In fact, one can conclude nothing about them if the only datum is that one variant of capitalism is faulted. Further, from *Populorum Progressio*'s early paragraphs Rand—who, as the proponent of an ideology allegedly based on reason and nothing else, should have known better—should have (rightly) concluded that if only certain kinds of capitalism are faulted, then others must be all right under Catholic social doctrine.

The encyclical did not fault capitalism for its essentials (profit, competition, private production). It faulted the idea that profit is the primary, the key, even the only motive for economic progress. The key motive should not be personal gain but the common good and the desire to have a sufficiency of goods so one's mind can turn to God. Also faulted was the idea that "competition is the supreme law of economics." Competition cannot be an absolute rule since it will degenerate into power grabs and exploitation. Taken far enough, it will, on its own, produce a life that is "solitary, poor, nasty, brutish, and short"—the classic "might makes right" situation.

The encyclical rejected the idea that private ownership of the means of production is an absolute right. It is a high right, but the demands of justice are higher. The needs of the common good are higher. Rand mistakenly assumed that the only alternative to an absolute right is no right at all and a take-over of productive capacity by the state. The problem is where to draw the line, and such applications of abstract ethics to concrete situations are difficult. As the necessity to relinquish ownership becomes less strong, the right to keep property in a particular circumstance becomes more strong. Only when there is absolutely no necessity in justice to give up ownership can there be, vis-à-vis a particular situation, an "absolute" right to maintain ownership.

Leaving these considerations, Rand maintained that the "most specific accusation directed at capitalism" concerned greed, but this criticism was not aimed solely at capitalism. It applies to all situations in which wealth is produced and distributed. Greed is a frequent visitor when the door of production is opened, for some of a good excites people's appetites for more. Greed is common among rich and poor. "Individuals, families, or nations can be overcome by avarice, be they rich or poor, and all can fall victim to a stifling materialism." With these words from the encyclical we can see that Rand was just plain wrong when she claimed Paul VI was aiming his document at the rich only.

She noted that the personal consumption of the rich is small, as a proportion of their wealth. True. But greed and avarice are manifested in hoarding and frivolous use. Beyond this, Rand failed to see the connection between irresponsibility in the economic sphere and irresponsibility in the political. For her the two were entirely separate, but, in all countries, in all of history, greater economic power has gone hand in hand with greater political power. "The insatiable desire for more" generally, though not always, leads to both powers. After all, although economic power may be identified with the production of goods—and this is what Rand did—the use or application of these goods is a form of political power. This she neglected to see.

Consider the case of the English nobles who acquired monastic land from Henry VIII. As Belloc related, the more land they received, the more the nobles sought power and privilege from the King. As they obtained from him political and economic privileges, they began taking over the lands of the peasantry, who, prior to that time, for the most part owned their own small parcels. This process of the large devouring the small reversed only in the nineteenth century when the peasants-turned-proletarians (property-less citizens) by sheer number applied pressure to the Commons.

Going even further, Rand claimed that the encyclical damned the ambition to expand productive capacity. What was condemned, though, was the call for a purely materialistic development. Pope Paul said that "if further development calls for . . . more technicians, even more necessary [is] authentic development," which is only secondarily material and firstly spiritual. Expansion of economic production is a good in itself (environmental hazards and other externalities aside), but it is insufficient alone.

It is interesting that Milton Friedman came to Ayn Rand's aid in misinterpreting what the Holy Father said. In a column appearing shortly after the encyclical was released, Friedman complained that the Pope's suggestions would not, in fact, produce the most goods for the most people. Maybe not. The point was not the amount of goods produced, but production in conjunction with higher goods. It is better to have a society informed by charity with some loss to production than to have a charityless society that produces an uncountable number of goods. The whole purpose of our human society is to prepare us for that better society we hope to attain. Material goods are of inferior importance to moral, ethical, and social goods. The latter kinds may be easier to secure if we have at least some of the former, yet, if we have nothing but the former, an efficient yet virtueless society, then we have not moved closer to heaven.

Ayn Rand looked at things differently. "The encyclical's principle is clear: Only those who rise no higher than the barest minimum of subsistence have the right to material possessions—and this right supersedes all the rights of all other men, including their right to life." To substantiate this, she quoted paragraph 22, but this says that all rights are subordinate to the demands of charity and that a person cannot obey the second great commandment if selfishness precludes his helping others. God's intention is for the earth to be shared and enjoyed by all, and men are expected to fulfill his will before their own.

The encyclical quoted Ambrose: "Private property does not constitute for anyone an absolute and unconditional right. No one is justified in keeping for his exclusive use what he does not need, when others lack necessities." Rand complained that this ignored the maker of the "created goods." She argued that the man who "creates" something should hold entire rights over it. True "creation," though, implies *ex nihilo*, and no man can create in that sense. The Artificer of "created goods" is the Father, and

so he has an inalienable lien on all created goods and all transformed goods into which they are made. The property rights of
men are like bailee rights: Much can be done with the property,
but it cannot be destroyed. It cannot be right for a legal owner,
say, to destroy his lake by pouring in it deadly pollutants. He has
the right to use the lake if his use does not harm others and if it
is in accord with God's will, but he has no absolute right since
he himself is only a creature. (Besides, the lake is likely to outlast
him and many other owners by countless ages.)

Men at best transform created goods, and it is this transformation that gives the owner certain rights superior to those of
other individuals. First, the transformation is an expenditure of
part of the man; he is used up to effect the transformation. Second,
he becomes united metaphysically with his property. As Richard
Weaver, the cultural critic, said, "It must be maintained that property is needed to help him express his being, his true or personal
being. By some mystery of imprint and assimilation man becomes
identified with his things, so that a forcible separation of the two
seems like a breach in nature." The right a man thus gets is superior to those of other individuals, but inferior to the common
good. It is absolutely inferior to God, against whom no one has
a claim.

Back to the quotation from Ambrose. Rand said in response
that "Ambrose lived in the fourth century, when such views of
property could conceivably have been explicable, if not justifiable.
From the nineteenth century on they can be neither." But views
on property do not depend on scientific advances. They do not
depend on the calendar. They depend on philosophy. With im-
proved science we now understand that life begins at fertilization,
not at the much later quickening, as some people once thought.
This does not alter the Christian view of the sacredness of life
—it merely allows us to appreciate the sacredness sooner. The
philosophy is not changed.

G. K. Chesterton, in *Orthodoxy*, put it well:

> An imbecile habit has arisen in modern controversy of saying that
> such and such a creed can be held in one age but cannot be held
> in another. Some dogma, we are told, was credible in the twelfth

century but is not credible in the twentieth. You might as well say that a certain philosophy can be believed on Mondays but cannot be believed on Tuesdays. You might as well say of a view of the cosmos that it was suitable to half-past three but not suitable to half-past four. What a man can believe depends upon his philosophy, not upon the clock or the century.

If a philosophic position on private property was correct in the fourth century, so also is it correct in the twentieth or twenty-first.

Rand next turned to the solutions the encyclical offered to the problems of the world. She concluded that the Church backs some vague sort of totalitarianism. The encyclical said that

> programs are in order "to encourage, stimulate, coordinate, supplement, and integrate" the activities of individuals and of intermediary bodies. It pertains to the public authorities to choose, even to lay down, the objectives to be pursued, the ends to be achieved, and the means for attaining these, and it is for them to stimulate all the forces engaged in this common activity.

The encyclical then cautioned that prudence must be used when the authorities design programs for development.

> But let them take care to associate private initiative and intermediary bodies with this work. They will thus avoid the danger of complete collectivization or of arbitrary planning, which, by denying liberty, would prevent the exercise of the fundamental rights of the human person.

In other words, the government may take a hand in solving or at least coordinating solutions to major social problems, but it should retain its rightful place and should not usurp the prerogatives of either individuals or of those intermediary bodies like the family, the Church, guilds and unions, and fraternal organizations. This statement, of course, left much leeway—different countries, or even different parts of the same country, may use different proportions and combinations of government and private power, and the system to be employed depends upon a nation's culture, traditions, and economic and social development. An economically backward country based on the tribal system will have needs differing from those of a moderately industrialized country with a strong rural identity or of a highly industrialized country with much social atomization.

Ayn Rand did not understand this. She concluded that since the government was said to have some sort of role, that the government must do—or try to do—everything. "A society in which the government . . . chooses and lays down the ends to be achieved, and the means for achieving them, is a totalitarian state." She insisted on taking things to extremes, for she ignored the caveat about denying liberty; she forgot that the encyclical was talking about the public and private sectors fulfilling their proper roles. "What is incomplete collectivization?" she asked in reply to the Pope's statement that giving the individual and the intermediary bodies their proper roles will "avoid the danger of complete collectivization."

Rand shifted the focus of her attack by turning to ethics. "Here again, the encyclical confirms my statements ('that every political theory is based on some code of ethics'), though from a viewpoint of a moral code which is the opposite of mine." After quoting the encyclical's statement that rich nations have an obligation to help poor nations, Rand quoted part of paragraph 58: "In other words, the rule of free trade, taken by itself, is no longer able to govern international relations. . . . One must recognize that it is the fundamental principle of liberty, as the rule for commercial exchange, which is questioned here." From this she concluded that the encyclical said that no man has a right to more than a minimum subsistence and that poor nations may claim everything a rich nation produces above the subsistence level. "If need—global need—is the criterion of morality, if minimum subsistence (the standard of living of the least developed savages) is the criterion of property rights, then every new dress or shirt, every ice-cream cone, every automobile, refrigerator, or television set becomes 'superfluous wealth.'"

To understand what was going on here, we must fill in the gap in the quotation Rand gave us. Here is the complete quotation:

> In other words, the rule of free trade, taken by itself, is no longer able to govern international relations. Its advantages are certainly evident when the parties involved are not affected by any excessive

inequality of economic power: It is an incentive to progress and a reward for effort. That is why industrially developed countries see it as a law of justice. But the situation is no longer the same when economic conditions differ too widely from country to country: Prices which are "freely" set in the market can produce unfair results. One must recognize that it is the fundamental principle of liberty, as the rule for commercial exchange, which is questioned here.

By filling in the gap we can understand what paragraph 58 meant. In cases in which one nation, because of its superior bargaining position, can take advantage of another, "the rule of free trade, taken by itself, is no longer able to govern." Something else must be added to the rule of free trade, and this is Christian charity. This principle, with a secularized "fairness" substituted for charity, is recognized in Anglo-American law in the unconscionable contract situation. If a man with a canteen of water happens upon a nearly dead fellow in the desert and offers to sell the thirsting man a drink if he will sign over all his wealth, courts will not uphold the contract. They will declare it void as against public policy. In such a situation "the rule of free trade is no longer able to govern." Charity, or at least a sense of fair play, must be taken into consideration.

Much the same thing may happen "when economic conditions differ too widely from country to country: Prices which are 'freely' set in the market can produce unfair results." The present agricultural plight of sub-Saharan Africa is so severe that a nation with an abundance of food could, with a little hard sell, buy up the rights to portions of those countries lock, stock, and locusts, for just a few shipments of wheat. To do so would be to have the market mechanism supersede Christian principles. It is these principles, said Rand, that form "a moral code which is the opposite of mine." It is an understanding of these that makes it untenable to conclude, as she did, that poor nations have a right to all a rich nation produces above the subsistence level. Although poor nations have no legal right to these goods, their suffering provides them a moral claim on rich nations—a moral claim that insists on the fulfillment of charitable obligations. To take from the rich everything but bare subsistence is quite different from recognizing that the rich must use their riches wisely. Over the centuries the needle's eye has not grown any larger nor the camel any smaller.

Yet Rand remained obstinate. She saw merely that some men's acquisitive appetites may not be satisfied if spirit is put above flesh (and in this she was right). A denial of the preeminent place of the appetites she found not only philosophically unsound but also cruel:

> It is not possible that Pope Paul VI was so ignorant of economics and so lacking in the capacity to concretize his theories [not the Church's 'theories,' but the Pope's alone] that he offered such pro-posals in the name of 'humanism' [not in the name of the Church] without realizing the unspeakably inhuman cruelty they entail. It seems inexplicable. But there is a certain basic premise that would explain it. It would integrate the encyclical's clashing elements—the contradictions, the equivocations, the omissions, the unanswered questions—into a consistent pattern. To discover it, we must ask: What is the encyclical's view of man's nature?

She concluded that the Pope's view of man's nature was one of "nameless fear"—this was the "sense of life that produced the encyclical *Populorum Progressio*. It was not produced by the sense of life of any one person but by the sense of life of an institution," and this institution, the Church, is fearful of new ideas. Indeed, said Rand, "the dominant chord of the encyclical's sense of life is hatred for man's mind—hence hatred for man—hence hatred for life and for this earth—hence hatred for man's enjoyment of life on this earth—and hence, as a last and least consequence, hatred for the only social system that makes all these values possible in practice: capitalism." She continued: "There is no place for the mind in the world proposed by the encyclical and no place for man. The entities populating it are sentient robots geared to per-form prescribed tasks in a gigantic tribal machine, robots deprived of choice, judgment, values, convictions, and self-esteem."

Rand moved next to a consideration of the encyclical's guide-lines for assisting undeveloped countries. She rebelled against the papal injunction that emissaries to the countries conduct themselves in a spirit of "brotherly love," understanding and appreciating both their own limitations and the great cultural and human worth to be found wherever they may go.

> This is said to civilized men who are to venture into countries where sacred cows are fed, while children are left to starve—where female infants are killed or abandoned by the roadside—where men go blind, medical help being forbidden by their religion—where women are mutilated, to insure their fidelity—where unspeakable tortures are ceremoniously inflicted on prisoners—where cannibalism is practiced. Are these the "cultural riches" which a Western man is to greet with "brotherly love"?

The Christian answer: Yes, even the holders of these beliefs, the practitioners of these rites, the inflicters of these tortures are to be greeted with "brotherly love"—plus a good dose of these spiritual works of mercy: admonishment of sinners and instruction of the ignorant.

Ayn Rand misunderstood the duties of the Christian; she produced at best a facile half-truth. The Christian emissary to these countries "is not to judge, not to question, not to condemn—only to love, to love without cause, indiscriminately, unconditionally, in violation of any values, standards, or convictions of his own." But these are not mutually exclusive demands. Injustice is to be condemned, but even the unjust are to be loved. Ignorance is to be replaced with understanding, but even the ignorant are to be respected. True values are to be raised against false, but even those in error are to be greeted with the words Christ spoke to the adulteress: "Go your way, and from now on sin no more." Rand, to put it simply, was incapable of understanding Mother Teresa.

She could see no use for brotherly love. "The only valuable assistance Western man could, in fact, offer to undeveloped countries is to enlighten them on the nature of capitalism and help them to establish it." This reminds one of what Malcolm Muggeridge had to say:

Now, we who are sated, who have to adopt the most extravagant and ridiculous devices to consume what we produce, while watching whole, vast populations getting hungrier and hungrier, overcome our feelings of guilt by persuading ourselves that these others are too numerous, have too many children. They ask for bread and we give them contraceptives!

Were the sentiments of Ayn Rand much different? She thought about the long-run and said, Give them a more efficient economic system, and a generation from now there will be food for all. The modern man against whom Muggeridge wrote says, Give them the pill, and a generation from now there will be fewer of them and so food for all. What is to happen until this wondrous transformation occurs? Should we just kick aside the living corpses because, after all, it is their own fault if they are too stupid to adopt the right economic system or if they live under despotic little governments that misallocate resources on purpose?

Paul VI did not think that "the only valuable assistance that Western man could, in fact, offer to undeveloped countries is to enlighten them on the nature of capitalism," at least not Ayn Rand's brand of capitalism. In fact, he even suggested that entrepreneurs from industrialized countries should not take advantage of the underdeveloped peoples. "It happens," said the Pope, that industrialists, merchants, and leaders of larger enterprises

are not lacking in social sensitivity in their own country, why then do they return to the inhuman principles of individualism when they operate in less developed countries? Their advantaged situation should on the contrary move them to become the initiators of social progress and of human advancement in the area where their business calls them. Their very sense of organization should suggest to them the means for making intelligent use of the labor of the indigenous population, of forming qualified workers, of training engineers and staffs, of giving scope to their initiative, of introducing them progressively to higher positions, thus preparing them to share, in the near future, in the responsibilities of management. At least let justice always rule the relations between superiors and their subordinates. Let standard contracts govern these relationships. Finally, let no one, whatever his status, be subjected unjustly to the arbitrariness of others.

It is to this attitude that Pope Paul contrasted "the inhuman principles of individualism." To this contrast Rand made no reference; she said only: "Observe that the horrors of tribal existence in those undeveloped countries evoke no condemnation from the encyclical; only individualism—the principle that raised mankind out of the primordial swamps—is branded as 'inhuman.'" (It may be beside the point to note that there is virtually no "tribal existence" in Latin America, most of Asia, and even much of Africa— let alone "tribal existence" with "horrors," which, for Rand, presumably meant cannibalism and head shrinking. Besides, mankind left the primordial swamps, if ever it was there, long before the ideology of individualism arose in the nineteenth century.)

Pope Paul said more than this. He said, "The younger or weaker nations are to assume their active part in the construction of a better world, one which shows deeper respect for the rights and the vocation of the individual." To which Rand asked: "What are the rights of the individual in a world that regards individualism as 'inhuman'?" Her question betrayed her failure to understand that the sanctity of the individual is not best guaranteed by the ideology of individualism; in fact, in the long run individualism secures the triumph of the collective. To show this we will have to make a detour.

According to Fr. Walter Brugger's *Philosophical Dictionary*, individualism is

> the name given to the view of society that so stresses the value of the individual that society turns out to be only the sum of the individuals, but not a real whole or unity. The rights and freedom of the individual in this view are supposed to be limited only by the very same rights of the other person and not by an inner relationship to the community.

What this ideology necessitates—what we have seen happen during the last century—is the gradual withering of subsidiary institutions: the workman's guild (now replaced by powerful and privileged unions), the local association, the family, the fraternal club, the charitable society, even the Church in her social role. Where individualism exerts a large influence these intermediary groups decline in importance, leaving atomized and alienated individuals confronting the state. This situation leads to collectivism, which stands in contrary opposition (not in contradiction) to individualism. Collectivism is individualism writ large. Collectivism makes just as much an absolute out of the collective as individualism does of the individual.

Under individualism, frustrated and alienated individuals cannot turn to the nonexistent intermediate societies for community or help. They can turn only to the state, which then necessarily oversteps its rightful bounds as it tries to become father, brother, and guardian. As it tries to do what it cannot do well, the state becomes increasingly despotic. This tendency toward collective tyranny is one element of individualism. It alone would warrant condemnation, but there is another error in this ideology. It leaves no room for God. To do that would be to de-absolutize the individual and to admit limits on individual actions, even when such actions "do not harm others."

Here Rand made the connection between religion (she used the term "mysticism") and what she called altruism: "The encyclical is the manifesto of an impassioned hatred for capitalism, but its evil is much more profound and its target is more than mere politics. It is written in terms of a mystic-altruist 'sense of life.'" So she finally came to her chief bugaboo, altruism, "the creed of self-sacrifice—the primordial weapon used to penalize man's success on earth, to undercut his self-confidence, to cripple his independence, to poison his enjoyment of life, to emasculate his pride, to stunt his self-esteem and paralyze his mind." It is altruism that seeks to limit man's pride through sacrifice for the welfare of others. Since religion rests on altruism, its main accomplishment is the neglect of the self and the promotion of others. Yet "the relief of suffering is not altruism's motive; it is only its rationalization. Self-sacrifice is not altruism's means to a happier end, it is its end—self-sacrifice as man's permanent state, as a way of life."

There is no reason to come to altruism's rescue just because it was attacked. Altruism is not the basis of Catholicism, as Rand implied. It is not a part of it at all, for altruism is the humanitarian's charity—a charity without the love of God as a motivating force. Charity is the great theological virtue, not altruism, and when a Christian acts charitably toward another, he does so first for the greater glory of God (following the first great commandment) and then for the welfare of his fellow in order to show further his love for God (following the second great commandment). So no defense of altruism is needed. Yet, through her attack on it, Rand really attacked the Catholic Church by implication, and this is what should be borne in mind. It was a matter of guilt by association.

She next discussed what political system the encyclical advocated. "It would, apparently, find any political system acceptable provided it is a version of statism. The vague allusions to some nominal form of private property make it probable that the encyclical favors fascism. On the other hand, the tone, style, and vulgarity of argumentation suggest a shopworn Marxism." (So much for her reading of *Mit Brennender Sorge* and *On Atheistic Communism*.) What is the motive for the Church to push some sort of totalitarianism? Why, it is an example of religion's "desperate attempt to recapture the power it lost at the time of the Renaissance. . . . The Catholic Church has never given up the hope to reestablish the medieval union of Church and State, with a global theocracy as its ultimate goal."

The Church is not to be excoriated only for desiring once more to exert a profound influence on men. She must also be found guilty of once almost capturing reason and then letting it go.

Catholicism had once been the most philosophical of all religions. Its long, illustrious philosophical history was illuminated by a giant: Thomas Aquinas. He brought an Aristotelian view of reason (an Aristotelian epistemology) back into European culture and lighted the way to the Renaissance. For the brief span of the nineteenth cen-

tury, when his was the dominant influence among Catholic philoso-
phers, the grandeur of his thought almost lifted the Church close to
the realm of reason (though at the price of a basic contradiction).

This trend toward reason—as though reason had never had any
home in the Church before the nineteenth century—was not to
last long. "Now, we are witnessing the end of the Aquinas line
—with the Church turning again to his primordial antagonist,
who fits it better, to the mind-hating, life-hating St. Augustine."
Rand's rhetoric served only to confuse. Although Augustine and
Thomas had different emphases (the first centered his writings,
such as *The City of God*, on the will; the second looked more
to faith), they were complementary parts of the whole. Beyond
that, Augustine, like Thomas, was a skilled logician. Read in *The
City of God* his chapters concerning how Cain could have been
said to have founded a city when, in fact, he was himself only
of the second generation. Or look at Augustine's consideration
of the great spans of those early lives and whether it would be
sensible to say that the Genesis years must have been only a tenth
the length of modern years. Here Augustine makes exquisite use
of the syllogism and the principle of contradiction.

Rand leaves these saints quickly—she throws them in only for
sparks—and immediately gets to her peroration: "It's either-or. If
capitalism's befuddled, guilt-ridden apologists do not know it, two
fully consistent representatives of altruism do know it: Catholicism and communism." (What they know—something she never
seemed to appreciate—is that the capitalist system cannot stand
for long without a moral base.)

> Their rapprochement, therefore, is not astonishing. Their differ-
> ences pertain only to the supernatural, but here, in reality on earth,
> they have three cardinal elements in common: the same morality,
> altruism—the same goal, global rule by force—the same enemy,
> man's mind.

In response one could note that neither Catholicism nor communism has altruism as the basis of its moral system; that, while
communism certainly wants to achieve global rule by force, the

kind of rule the Church looks for is the kind of obedience one would expect to obtain spontaneously from people who are confronted with the Son of their Creator; and that neither system has man's mind as an enemy but that communism wants to "improve" that mind ideologically and Catholicism wants it to perceive its true relations to faith and God.

"Well, as a friend of mine observed," closed Rand, "only the Vatican, the Kremlin, and the Empire State Building know the real issues of the modern world." There is, admittedly, much to be said for the juxtaposition of the first two. After all, as Erik von Kuehnelt-Leddihn said, "the efforts to draw comparisons between the Vatican and the Kremlin are usually made in the spirit of hostility, but they are not without substance if we bear in mind that the various *isms*, as fundamental heresies, are indeed evil caricatures of fragments of Christian doctrine, of Christian institutions." It is less than clear that the Empire State Building—where Rand had her headquarters—has much to say in defense of true freedom or about the real issues of the modern world—or, for that matter, about the kind of free market that is compatible with Christian social principles. Ayn Rand may be dead, but her bad ideas have not gone to the grave with her. Buyer beware.

II

The By-Your-Own-Bootstraps Heretic

Beginning his life with the given name of Morgan, this future heresiarch was known by the Romans as "the man of the sea," Pelagius. He was born in Britain around 354, the year Augustine, his great opponent, was born at Tagaste in Numidia. His British birth is partly deduced from his cognomen of Britannicus and from the fact that a town in Wales has long claimed to be his birthplace. Jerome, perhaps in anticipation of Samuel Johnson's ribbing of James Boswell's national origin, ridiculed Pelagius as a Scot who, "stuffed with Scottish porridge," suffered from a weak memory. It may have been that the "Scots" of those days were really the Irish, in which case Pelagius's true home is to be found in Ireland.

Pelagius was tall and fat ("*grandis et corpulentus,*" said Jerome) and was well educated, speaking and writing both Latin and Greek; although extremely polemical in nature, he was trenchant and concise as a writer. Never a priest, he was a monk devoted to practical asceticism. In Rome he enjoyed a reputation of austerity, and Augustine even called him a saintly man. Beyond this, little is known of his early years. He came to Rome either between 380 and 384 under Pope Anastasius, at which time he was baptized, or between 375 and 380 during the first years of Gratian. In all likelihood he studied law. While in the capital he composed several works that were termed by Gennadius "indispensable reading matter for students." Some of his writings formerly were attributed to Augustine, Jerome, and other orthodox scholars. Only three have been preserved in their entirety. Fragments of still other early works of his are preserved in the writings of his opponents.

When Rome fell in 410, Pelagius sought refuge at Carthage. With him was his close friend and collaborator, Caelestius, who remained there hoping to become a priest. Caelestius was not able to have himself ordained in Carthage, "as he had imbibed and taught more openly than Pelagius the latter's heresy." So said Louisa Cozens in her *Handbook of Heresies*. Caelestius went on to Ephesus and was ordained there, the Ephesians evidently being more open-minded, or themselves perhaps less orthodox, than the Carthaginians. For his part, Pelagius traveled on to Jerusalem, which became his home until 418, after which point there is no further information about him. (In *The Faith of the Early Fathers* William Jurgens makes this safe statement: "Pelagius disappears from history after 418 and has long since been presumed dead." One would hope so.)

In Jerusalem Pelagius became friends with the bishop, John, who befriended him against accusations by Orosius and some Latin exiles. At this time Pelagius was a leader of the Origenist party in Jerusalem. Origen (185–254), the most prolific of early Christian writers (he was said to have written 800 works, but few of them survive), had attempted to synthesize Christianity with Neoplatonism and Stoicism, but he was not particularly successful. He was unreliable, at times heterodox; he favored, for instance, the *apokatastasis*, the notion that in the end even hell will dissolve and all creatures, including damned men and angels, will be saved and united with God in heaven. Controversies arising from his teachings lasted centuries longer than did the leaves of paper that enshrined most of his writings. As a partisan of Origen, Pelagius seems to have been schooled in less-than-orthodox thinking. He was ripe for trouble.

In 415 charges were brought against him at Diospolis, the ancient city of Lydda, based on six propositions culled from his works. His accusers were two exiled Gallic bishops, Heros of Arles and Lazarus of Aix. Pelagius's propositions affirmed the real possibility of man's impeccability (capacity not to sin). This possibility arose out of man's free will, which, Pelagius asserted, could be so guided as to permit man always to obey God's commandments. Pelagius distanced himself from Caelestius, who was less the politician, and spoke in terms of a theoretical, as distinguished from a practical, possibility of impeccability, and he either denied teaching the more clearly heretical doctrines or offered orthodox explanations. (Yet Augustine quotes Pelagius as saying, "I teach that it is possible for men to live without sin"—a blunt, unequivocal line.)

Pelagius was helped by the fact that his accusers failed to show up for the hearing, and he took advantage of Eastern Christians' unfamiliarity with these issues. Thus he avoided condemnation at Diospolis. After his acquittal, which his supporters took to be a vindication of his theses themselves, Pelagius wrote a self-justifying piece, which a deacon from Hippo, Carus, sent to Augustine. The great duel was joined.

Before considering further the interplay of the personalities, we should examine in more detail Pelagius's theological system. Much of its appeal lay in his zeal. He preached against the lukewarm moralism that was then common, and stricter Christians found his sermons popular. (Here we see a foreshadowing of the appeal of present-day Fundamentalism, which may be weak theologically but is strong morally—and therefore attractive.) The moral attractiveness was joined with another kind, the denial of original sin. Historian Jean-Remy Palanque noted that

> Pelagianism was based on a very respectable moral rigorism, but its anxiety to champion man's free will and to urge him on to sanctity resulted in its denying original sin and the necessity of divine grace: For the Pelagian, access to the Kingdom is made possible by baptism, and since perfect sanctity is an obligation and a possibility for everyone, it rests with each individual Christian to merit eternal life by his conduct, modeled on the precepts and example of Christ.

According to Pelagius the human will is free and is equally capable of choosing good or evil. "God, desiring to endow the rational creature with the function of voluntary goodness and the power of free will, and by implanting in man the possibility of both, makes it man's special character that he wills, so that he is naturally capable of both good and evil, and he may be inclined to the willing of either." This freedom would be destroyed if the will were inclined to evil for any reason (or to good, for that matter). Grace is entirely external and merely facilitates what the will can do on its own. Grace is a help, not a necessity.

From such considerations Pelagius drew certain conclusions.

Adam's sin was purely personal, and it therefore would have been unjust for God to punish the entire human race for Adam's sin. Since God is not unjust, he did not so punish us, and this suggests death is not a punishment handed down from the first man but is a necessary part of human nature. It would have been with us even if Adam had not sinned. Other disabilities conventionally associated with Adam's sin could not have been imposed as punishments, and this meant there could have been no primitive paradise because Adam's personal sin could not have lost it, and concupiscence, the existence of which Pelagius did not deny, must have been part of the human make-up from the first. In this Pelagius agreed with Julian of Eclanum, who, reported Augustine, claimed that concupiscence was created by God together with the body and that only a Manichaean would see it as an evil and a consequence of sin. Since Adam's sin was personal, argued Pelagius, everyone is born sinless, there being no such thing as original sin. (In modern parlance, we are all immaculately conceived.) This makes infant baptism useless; a child, being incapable of sin, needs no washing away of sin, and an infant who dies goes immediately to heaven. Baptism should be reserved for adults.

Then why, one might ask, is sin so prevalent? Pelagius speculated that, from childhood, we contract the habit of sinning, and this habit becomes second nature. The newborn child is as pure as Adam and Eve at their creation, but, as he advances in age, the child learns to sin from those around him. Specifically, he learns from the bad examples of his elders, and then he becomes a bad example himself. If he were isolated from the "contagion," he could grow into a sinless adult, but no one grows up in complete isolation. Pelagius's problem, wrote Joseph Tixeront in his *History of Dogmas*, is that "he saw only guilty individuals, not a whole sinful human race." Since the human race does not labor under original sin or any other consequences of the Fall (since the Fall affected only Adam and Eve), there was no need for redemption as such—there was nothing to be redeemed from. Why did Christ come then? To give us an example, to be a role model. Adam was the bad role model, Christ the good.

Even before Christ there were men who lived sinless lives, said Pelagius. This seems to be a necessary, even an inescapable, consequence of his teaching. It would hardly do to say that, although men always have been able to live sinlessly, not a single one has. Pelagius does not seem to have claimed that any particular individuals after the appearance of Christ lived sinless lives—at least he did not make that claim for himself. Anyway, if sinlessness had occurred before the time of Christ, it could be the state of mankind again.

From what Catholic historian Newman Eberhardt has indicated, it would seem that Pelagius would not have been the confessor of choice for many people:

> As spiritual director, he became tired of hearing men excuse themselves for sin and tepidity on the plea of human frailty. To such alibis he gradually developed the retort that these were but excuses for indolence [and that] every man is quite capable of perfection by his own efforts provided that he only apply them to action.

Here we have a foreshadowing, perhaps, of today's "power of positive thinking."

The upshot of this system was the elimination of any need for grace. God takes no active role in human salvation, since men do not need his grace; he is, instead, something of a spectator, watching the human drama from afar but not involving himself in it after setting it on its course. We see in Pelagianism a kind of early Deism: The divine clock maker winds up the universe and then leaves it alone.

Pelagius lived in an era when grace was still vague and undefined. Not even another millennium proved to be enough time for the doctrine of grace to be worked out fully—consider the seventeenth-century heresy of Jansenism, merely one example of continuing confusions. In Pelagius's time it was generally understood that some sort of assistance was necessary for salvation and was given freely by God, but the nature of that assistance had not been thought out rigorously. Pelagius thought about it and concluded the assistance did not exist.

To Caelestius must go much of the credit (or blame, however one sees it) for the spread of Pelagianism. Without him the heresy may have been short-lived and of modest effect. An untiring propagandist, he was its principal exponent. Even though his real beliefs were demonstrated in debates as early as 411 by adversaries such as Paulinus, Caelestius's position advanced. He tried to transform the practical maxims learned from Pelagius into theoretical principles, and it was these he propagated.

The battle against Pelagianism was waged on several fronts. The greatest champion of the orthodox cause was Augustine, who wrote fifteen treatises against Pelagianism and whose territory Pelagius and Caelestius had invaded on leaving the sacked capital. In 412 Augustine wrote two works that emphasized that man's will had been weakened through original sin and that that weakness made necessary God's help. In 417 he wrote an account of the council of Diospolis and showed that Pelagius had been forced to disavow some of what Caelestius had been teaching.

Augustine's position may be summarized this way: God created our first parents in a state of innocence and gave them supernatural and preternatural gifts, including infused knowledge and freedom from death and illness. They were "able not to sin." Despite these advantages, man fell, and by falling he lost the gifts. His state degenerated to one in which he was "not able not to sin." His redemption would come only with the Savior, the New Adam, who, being at once God and man, was "not able to sin."

Another opponent of Pelagianism was Orosius, a young Spanish priest sent by Augustine to Jerusalem to alert Jerome and the bishops there of the dangers of the heresy. This journey was made while Pelagius was being honored in Palestine, Caelestius having been excommunicated at Carthage before moving on to Ephesus.

In 415 Orosius and Pelagius appeared before a council of bishops at Jerusalem. The event was inconclusive, since Orosius knew little Greek and Pelagius, who was proficient in it, was able to sway the bishops by his equivocations. Bishop John referred the matter to Rome.

That very year Jerome—probably an octogenarian, but still intellectually active—entered the fray with two treatises against Pelagius and his followers: one a letter to Ctesiphon, the other called *Dialogus adversus Pelagianos*. It is said he weakened the force of his argument by that vituperativeness to which he was accustomed; by exaggerating Pelagius's claims, he undercut his own case. (From his misjudgment today's apologists should take a cue.)

When the bishops of Africa heard of the council of Diospolis, they thought it had given its approval to Pelagianism. In 416 councils convened at Carthage and Milevis; each council sent letters to Pope Innocent I, pointing out errors of the Pelagians and urging him to condemn Pelagius and Caelestius. Early the next year the Pope replied, approving what the bishops had done and excommunicating Pelagianism's two leaders. From Augustine's comments on this exchange of letters has come the maxim "Rome has spoken; the case is closed." But Augustine was mistaken. The case was not closed yet. Pelagius forwarded a profession of faith to Rome, and Caelestius went to the capital in person.

The struggle with Pelagianism then entered its Roman phase. In March 417 Innocent died. His successor was Zosimus. After reading Pelagius's profession of faith, he restored him to unity with the Church. As for Caelestius, the Pope wrote to the bishops of Africa, saying Heros and Lazarus had acted hastily and that the bishops either should exonerate Caelestius or should prove his heresy in the presence of the Pope. The letter, remarked historian Philip Hughes, "amounted to a panegyric of Pelagius and Caelestius, in which they figured as the calumniated victims of the malice of the bishops!" It should be noted that this incident cannot be used against the doctrine of papal infallibility, for two reasons: The letter by Zosimus does not meet the requirements for an infallible papal decree, as outlined at Vatican I, in that it is not a declaration made to the whole world, and Zosimus drew his conclusions based on Pelagius's confession of faith. At most Zosimus was saying that the confession of faith was orthodox; lacking convincing evidence to the contrary, Zosimus was bound to take the confession as an accurate representation of Pelagius's opinions.

The African bishops met in synod in November and composed a letter to Zosimus, asking him to withhold final disposition of the case until Pelagius and Caelestius had confessed the necessity of grace. By a rescript issued the next March, Zosimus said he had not yet pronounced definitively (this shows what his intentions were regarding whether the earlier letter was an exercise in infallibility—it could not have been, if he claimed not to be teaching definitively), and he forwarded to Africa all documents bearing on Pelagianism so a new investigation could be made. There followed a council at Carthage. The bishops again branded Pelagianism a heresy and affirmed the following points, among others, as elements of the true faith: Death came through sin; newborns must be baptized because of original sin; justifying grace assists the Christian in avoiding sin; grace imparts a strength of will to avoid sin; without grace meritorious good works are impossible; all men are sinners.

When the acts of the council were forwarded to Zosimus, he confirmed them in a letter in which he gave a summary of Pelagianism's history and errors and in which he renewed the excommunication of Pelagius and Caelestius. He ordered all bishops of the Church to sign the letter. When Theodotus, patriarch of Antioch, received the Pope's letter, he summoned a council, and Pelagius was expelled from Palestine and entirely disappeared from history. Caelestius refused to accept Rome's judgment but escaped punishment because of his protectors.

After 418 the leader of the Pelagians was Julian, bishop of Eclanum, said by commentators to have been pugnacious and a clever dialectician. He and seventeen other bishops of Italy declined to sign Zosimus's letter and insisted a general council be convened to reconsider the case afresh. All eighteen were excommunicated, deposed, and exiled, giving Julian the freedom to commence a literary war with Augustine. The two exchanged salvos repeatedly. Julian concluded that orthodoxy, as defined by Augustine and Zosimus, was something real Christians had to be rescued from. Dismissing his opponents in general as "uneducated and stupid" and Augustine as "that Punic preacher, dullest and most stupid of men," Julian, after being driven from Roman territory, found refuge in Cilicia with Theodore of Mopsuestia. After Theodore's death in 428, he went to Constantinople, and after that he too disappeared from history (and is also now presumed dead).

Pelagianism was not finally crushed in the East until the ecumenical Council of Ephesus, held in 431, confirmed the condemnation pronounced by the Western bishops. After Ephesus the heresy is almost unmentioned in the East, but it still smoldered in the West, its main centers being Gaul and (appropriately, since it was Pelagius's home) Britain. Not until the Second Council of Orange (529) did the heresy die out in the West, though that synod aimed its decisions at Semi-Pelagianism more than at Pelagianism outright. (The council declared, "If anyone maintains that the Fall harmed Adam alone and not his descendants, or declares that only bodily death, which is the punishment of sin, but not sin itself, which is the death of the soul, was passed on to the whole human race by one man, he ascribes injustice to God.")

Semi-Pelagianism did not arise only at the end of the struggle. Augustine had to deal with it a century earlier than did the bishops at Orange. He found himself forced to refute teachings of writers such as John Cassian, who repudiated Pelagianism in part but taught man was capable of making an initial act of faith without grace. Once in the state of justification, argued Semi-Pelagians, man needed supernatural grace to be saved, but no special grace to persevere. As a middle position, Semi-Pelagianism proved to have, in many ways, a popularity greater than Pelagianism itself enjoyed.

If it can be said that some good arises out of every evil, the good that arose out of Pelagianism was a study of original sin and the

Redemption and the affirmation that salvation is entirely gratuitous, that man can do nothing to earn salvation. Moderns are apt
to regard original sin as an outmoded consideration of theology,
but this attitude is by no means new. (It may, though, be peculiar
to our culture as a generalized motif.) More than three centuries
ago Pascal noted that "undoubtedly nothing offends us more than
this doctrine. And yet without this obscurest of all mysteries, we
are the greatest of enigmas to ourselves."

12

The Painted Word

Excavations in the Roman catacombs reveal that from the earliest times the Christian liturgy made use of sacred images. Crude likenesses of Christ and the martyrs of the Coliseum still may be traced on the walls of the burial chambers. As the Christian faith spread, so did the use of pictures of holy persons and symbols like the cross. The first recorded objections to images came from Xenias Philoxenius, Monophysite bishop of Mabboug. The Monophysites, a heretical sect of the fifth and succeeding centuries, deemed illicit any representation of Christ as man because they held that Christ had but one nature, the divine, not the human.

I am announced by the great door that slams closed behind me and sends echoes through the empty parish hall. From a side office emerges a young man of indeterminate age, his clerical collar telling me that I have found my guide. He extends his hand and introduces himself as the assistant to the pastor, and he seems pleased that a stranger wants to know more about the art and symbolism of this Greek Orthodox church. He apologizes straight away, saying that he may not be the best tour host because he is new to the area and has been ordained only a few weeks. He calls me "sir," as he will continue to address me throughout my visit; I am flattered and think to myself that the Greeks have not given up the fine art of civilizing their children.

As we leave the hall he notes that "basically, all over the world the Greek Orthodox Church is the same, in thought and in art." We make our way to the back of the church, going in through the priests' door, and in a few moments we are standing at the head of the main aisle, beneath a massive crystal chandelier, and he is pointing out the features of the iconostasis, or rood screen, the wall-like partition that separates the sanctuary from the nave.

At the end of the sixth century, Serenus, bishop of Marseilles, was rebuked by Gregory the Great for breaking church images, which, said Gregory, had been made "not for adoration, but merely for the promotion of reverence." Gregory reminded Serenus that "what Scripture is for those who can read, that a picture is for those who are incapable of reading." For a while the iconoclastic urge was controlled.

In a crisp but marked accent Father says that

in the Greek tragedy we always have the same scene. At the back of the stage is the royal palace, with three doors. The main door, in the center, is only for the royal family. The door at the left is for those coming into the city from the outside, as when a messenger comes with news of a battle. Through the right door enter the servants of the palace. The Greek tragedy, of course, originally served the purposes of religion—specifically, the worship of the god Dionysus. This had a strong influence in the Eastern Church,

and this influence may be found in the design of the present-day iconostasis.

This partition maintains the three doors of the Greek stage. (Appropriately enough, the liturgical ceremony is called the Divine Drama.) The middle door, through which the altar may be seen, is only for the priests and the bishops; no one else may pass through. The side doors are for the acolytes who twice during the liturgy walk in procession. The first procession comes at the reading of the Gospel and represents Christ entering Jerusalem in triumph on Palm Sunday. The second comes at the offertory and symbolizes Christ's journey from the Garden of Gethsemane to his condemnation before Pontius Pilate. Since both events began outside Jerusalem and ended within, the processions come into the view of the congregation through the left door of the iconostasis.

The iconostasis is more than just a backdrop for the processions; on its face are half a dozen large and finely detailed oils. The one over the left door is of Michael the Archangel; then come representations of the patron of the local church, the Virgin Mary, Christ, John the Evangelist, and, lastly, the Archangel Gabriel. Above these pictures are ornate lamps of bronze, and above the lamps are thirteen smaller paintings, each depicting a different event in the life of Christ. The painting astride the center door is the largest of the thirteen and is of the Last Supper; its interpretation is not unlike Leonardo da Vinci's. A large cross tops the iconostasis.

"The icon for us is not for decoration," emphasizes the priest. "Icons are books to be read by uneducated people." He points to the large, concave painting of the Virgin Mary that fills the wall behind and above the altar. "In our Church we say the Virgin Mary is the bridge by which God came to us; she is also the stairway for us to go to heaven. Therefore, her picture is always in the dome." Standing within the sanctuary, I see that the Virgin's arms, especially her fingers, are greatly elongated, no doubt for reasons of perspective. The congregation sees a normally proportioned image, but the priest, under the dome, surely must feel cradled by these encircling arms and hands, and that, too, seems appropriate.

Like the Monophysite Christians, the Muslims began a systematic policy of iconoclasm at the beginning of the eighth century, and this policy among his neighbors may have encouraged Leo the Isaurian, usurper of the Byzantine throne, in his war against images. He first showed his hostility by ordering workmen to destroy a popular icon in the Chalcopraetaia quarter of Constantinople, thereby precipitating 120 years of turmoil that would result—but not end—in a general council of the Church.

Father takes my arm and guides me to the center of the church. Turning up our heads we can view on the ceiling a massive painting of Jesus Christ Pantokratos, or Jesus Christ the Judge. I remark that in recent years there seems to have been a decided, though not official, trend in the Catholic Church to remove or downplay images, and I ask why no similar trend has been evident in the various Orthodox churches. "The Catholic Church does not keep the holy icons for education. They have the icons there for decoration. This is my personal opinion," explains Father, not needing to point out that when fashions change mere decorations change too.

> They don't have standards for the icons because there is no inten-
> tion that the icons will teach standard ideas. The Catholic Church
> just has paintings with religious themes. If you go into a Greek
> Orthodox church to see an icon of John the Evangelist, it is always
> the same. You always know which one he is. Remember, this is a
> copy of the book to be read by the uneducated.

Over the side doors are murals perhaps fifteen feet tall. The one on the right is of the woman at the well, and the one on the left portrays Christ as a boy teaching in the Temple. I ask about the painter, since everything seems to have been done by the same, skilled hand. "He was a man from Los Angeles, by the name of Savalas; he worked for Twentieth Century-Fox, but recently he died."

Along the arches and around the pictures are arabesques, evidence of the Islamic influence on the Eastern Church. In the older churches, particularly in Greece, the borders are always grape vines, which have Old Testament significance. The newer churches generally display geometrical designs.

For decades there flourished an iconoclastic schism within the Church. The General Council of Nicaea was called in 787 to condemn it, but the schism was prolonged by imperial rulers who used the religious troubles to gain political power over the West, which was rapidly slipping from the control of the Byzantine court. In 800 the political rift became complete with Pope Leo III's crowning of Charlemagne as Holy Roman Emperor.

We walk behind the iconostasis, and I find the priest holding an obviously old censer. Its four golden chains, he says, represent the four Gospels, and the twelve bells attached to the chains stand for the sermons of the twelve apostles. The cover, which can be raised, represents heaven, while the fixed base is the earth. "And this," says Father with a slight smile of embarrassment as he lifts out the incense holder from the middle, "is our little church, with the warm place of the people." He delights in a symbolism which some may think outdated. All these meanings, he continues, were written down by a sainted bishop of Salonika. "He wrote a book and explained everything in our Church. But in our days we don't often mention this symbolism, because some people do not understand. When this censer was made, with all these symbolic parts, it was made for a purpose and to give an explanation."

To the left of the altar, in a niche in the wall, are found the bread and wine that will be used in the consecration. Even the niche itself is symbolic; it is Bethlehem. "Everything starts from this place; this is the beginning." Over the ciborium, the vessel that will contain the consecrated Eucharist, is a star-shaped metal cover, the star of the magi.

Father points to a crucifix, noting that in the Greek representation Christ is never shown with blood or with a crown of thorns, and his fingers are always extended flat, never curved or clenched in pain. His body is not bent over, but he stands straight, as though he is holding up the cross. "This shows that he was not forced on the cross but put himself there voluntarily." The priest reminds me again that "everything in our Church is symbolic."

Icons of the Virgin are likewise more than mere representational accounts; they, too, are theological instructions. In Orthodox icons of the Crucifixion, the Virgin is never pictured collapsed on the ground, crying. In images of the Nativity she is always sitting up, never lying down, because she did not suffer labor pains. "In the Old Testament we learn that labor pains were one of the punishments for Adam's sin, but the Virgin Mary was not subject to that sin, so she was not subject to the punishments." Father gazes around the church and in a low voice says, "Everything is in the icons."

The Feast of Orthodoxy was first celebrated on the First Sunday in Lent, 843, and has given the Eastern Church its popular name. The Feast commemorates primarily the triumph of the iconodules over the iconoclasts. Since that time, the various Orthodox churches have refined the symbolism of the icons and have developed—and, through the centuries, maintained—that distinctive style of art known as Byzantine.

I mention to Father that I have at home a reproduction of a thirteenth-century Byzantine-style Madonna. He is clearly pleased and asks, "Do you want to see some old icons that I have?" We leave the church and walk next door to the white stucco house that will be his family's residence within a few weeks. Our footsteps resound throughout the empty rooms, and over the fireplace I see the three lonely occupants of the living room, icons of the Virgin, each painted on wood. "In the hallway there is one more," he says, leading me to the niche that in similar houses is for the telephone.

He sees that I am impressed and is emboldened to ask. "Do you want to see my prize icon, sir? I am told it is from the seventh century." We walk across the street to the hotel, his temporary lodgings, and he calls up to his room from the desk. But his wife is bathing their two young children (I can hear the howls even a few feet from the receiver), so I wait in the lobby while he mounts the elevator.

In a few minutes he returns, cradling in his hands a white terry-cloth towel, which he lays in his lap and carefully unfolds. Inside is an intricately carved wooden cross, protected by a silver casing, itself an example of master craftsmanship. "They destroyed it," says Father, referring to the fact that the silver had once been covered over with gold paint, perhaps to hide the icon's antiquity. The wooden cross itself, though one arm is broken and rattles within the casing, looks as though it were carved yesterday with the finest of tools and by a workman using a jeweler's glass. The front shows the Crucifixion and, at the end of the arms, the four Evangelists. The reverse portrays similar scenes.

The priest purchased the icon from a Russian refugee family in Switzerland.

I don't think they knew its value. My explanation is that if this belonged to that family through the generations, from father to son, they would not have sold it. After I bought it I showed it to a professor in Athens. He said, "Leave it with me a couple of days." When I went back, he confirmed that the wood is from the seventh century.

I took another look at the icon, a mere three inches high. Perhaps, I thought to myself, its small size saved it from Leo the Isaurian's bonfires and preserved it through the centuries until it found its way into the hands of this humble priest. It easily could have found a less loving caretaker.

13

The Faith in Old Japan

The small party of missionaries left Goa for Malacca, where the only available passage was on a Chinese pirate junk. This they took to Kagoshima, which lay at the southern end of Kyushu in a protected bay. Once the junk dropped anchor, Francis Xavier and two other Jesuits stepped ashore. It was the Feast of the Assumption, 1549, and it was the start of a century-long missionary effort that would end in gory martyrdoms, wholesale apostasies, and the apparent extinction of Christianity in Japan.

Shortly after his arrival, Xavier wrote to his superiors, saying that "the people we have met so far are the best yet discovered, and it seems to me that we shall never find among the heathens another race equal to the Japanese." But within two years he had concluded that the conversion of Japan depended on the prior conversion of China, which the Japanese considered as having a superior culture. When Xavier left in 1551, he was bid farewell by a thousand converts, only about half of whom were still in the faith when other Jesuits replaced him a few years later.

The political map of Japan in the middle of the sixteenth century was not unlike that of feudal Europe or of the Germanies even into the nineteenth century. Disorder was rampant; contemporary chronicles are full of petty wars among the *daimyos* (feudal lords) whose fiefs changed hands with monotonous regularity. The emperor was quite powerless, much as he is today, and what would become the national power was lodged in his generalissimo, the *shogun*, who operated from Kamakura, near Tokyo. The emperor was resident in Kyoto, Japan's second capital (the ancient capital, Nara, was some miles to the south), where he lived at a subsistence level, shorn of all pomp. When he needed extra funds, he sold titles to the *daimyos*, the monopoly on granting titles being his only source of wealth. Political unification of the country, accomplished during the last half of the sixteenth century and the first part of the seventeenth, came through the subjugation of the *daimyos* by the *shoguns*, three of whom are credited with accomplishing this task: Oda Nobunaga, Toyotomi Hideyoshi, and Tokugawa Ieyasu. It was said that Nobunaga mixed the dough, Hideyoshi baked it, and Ieyasu ate it, for Ieyasu's descendants, the Tokugawa clan, were to control Japan for the next two and a half centuries.

Each of these *shoguns* was, at one time or another, favorable to the missionaries; each in turn persecuted them and their converts. Their actions were based on temporal considerations, for none of the *shoguns* had any personal commitment to the faith. The Jesuits were tolerated because they were needed. Without them the Japanese could not arrange their commerce with the periodic merchant vessels and particularly with the great Portuguese carracks that once each year brought to Japan (and thus to the *shoguns*) new kinds of vast wealth. So long as the Jesuits were needed as intermediaries with the traders, Christianity spread, though in fits and starts. Once this need disappeared, the persecutions commenced in earnest.

The carracks, which sailed with the monsoons from Macao, were the largest ships afloat, displacing 1,600 tons. By the Japanese they were called *kurofune*, the black ships, because of the color of their hulls. In the early years they stopped at various ports, but from 1571 Nagasaki became the port of preference, partly because by then the local *daimyos* were Christians and partly because the harbor was well protected from both the elements and assault. It was here that the Jesuits chose to center their activities, and so Nagasaki became the hub of Japanese Christianity, as it would remain, even during the centuries of the Church of Silence, until on an August day in 1945 a tenth of all the Christians in Japan were killed at a stroke.

The rapidity of the conversions among the Japanese seems phenomenal, but, to the disappointment of hagiographers, this cannot be credited solely to the vigor of the missionaries. The Jesuits decided early that the technique most likely to succeed was to convert the *daimyos*, all of whose subjects would then instantly convert, as though under military orders. Things went largely according to this plan. There are accounts of as many as ten thousand conversions in a single day, all at a certain *daimyo*'s orders. Of course, there also were accounts of ten thousand un-conversions in a single day, when the *daimyo* turned on the Jesuits.

There were other complications. The Buddhist monks implacably opposed Christianity, not only from religious considerations but also because they feared that their temporal holdings, which would have been the envy of the most grasping European bishop, would be taken from them as Christianity advanced. The *shogun* Nobunaga was an agnostic, and among his bitterest enemies were the Buddhist bonzes who tended to support his political rivals and who even levied armies against him. The district around Kyoto, which with a population of about half a million was larger than any European city except perhaps Paris, was controlled by the military monks on Mount Hiei, which gives a commanding view of the great plain that runs from Kyoto to Osaka. Because the Buddhists were opposed by the Jesuits, Nobunaga often supported the latter.

Although most of the commoners at first followed their *daimyos* into the Church merely as a matter of course, many of them and of their descendants became fervent believers. The Jesuits concluded that of all Asians they encountered only the Japanese were capable of accepting the faith after rational demonstration and of leading devout lives. Since the Europeans never acquired a strong grasp of the language, and since there was never more than a handful of them in Japan at any one time, the real proselytizing was done by Japanese catechists, who traveled the length of the country and did not hesitate to use even the holy books of the Buddhists to dispute with them. As a rule, in Japan converts were held in high regard by their countrymen, unlike the situation in other Asian countries. But there were problems within the family. One was that the Europeans were slow in ordaining Japanese priests; several Japanese left the Jesuits when they saw no prospect of advancement. Some of the best Japanese apologists against the Buddhists apostatized and joined the opposition. The first two native priests were ordained only in 1602; when the final expulsion edict was issued a dozen years later, there were only five in the whole country, after more than sixty years of missionary effort.

Although the Jesuits were the first missionaries to Japan, they were not the only ones. A generation after Xavier's landing there arrived from Spanish-controlled Manila the first party of Franciscans. The Jesuits tried to convince Rome that competition between orders would give the Japanese the impression that Christianity, like Buddhism, was fissiparous, which would reduce the natives' respect for the new religion. Rome issued the necessary orders, but they were ignored in Manila. In came the friars and the *odium theologicum*.

The Franciscans and other mendicants who came after them took a different approach from the Jesuits. While the latter sought to convert the *daimyos* and the *samurai*, the former concentrated on the peasants. The friars wanted to erase the native culture and impose a European one, a technique that had proved successful in the Americas. While the Jesuits tried to blend in as much as possible with the surrounding culture, conscientiously adopting Japanese customs and even dress, the Franciscans flaunted their monastic habits, rosaries, and crosses, and they ignored many of the civilities. The double-track approach could have worked had not each side tried to belittle the other in the eyes of the *shoguns* and *daimyos*. The strife made the authorities all the more suspicious of the Europeans and all the more willing to believe the bonzes, who insisted that the missionary efforts were merely a front for impending invasions.

This suspicion soon appeared to be confirmed. Nobunaga and then Hideyoshi, in his early years as *shogun*, tolerated the missionaries reasonably well, till 1587, when the first blow fell. Some of Hideyoshi's retainers, after a night of carousing, regaled him with stories of forcible conversions by the Christians and the destruction of Shinto and Buddhist holy places by the new converts. Hideyoshi became enraged, despite his enmity with the Buddhists, and he issued the first of the expulsion orders, giving the priests twenty days to leave the country and ordering the removal of all Christian emblems from the dress of the *samurai* in his army. Much of the Jesuits' property was seized (the mendicants not yet having entered the country), and churches were closed or destroyed. But the actual expulsion was not carried out, though most of the missionaries ended up concentrated in the Nagasaki area. Hideyoshi, on reflection, understood that the expulsion of the Jesuits meant the end of the *kurofune* and the end of the wealth that gave him effective control of the country.

Ten years later came the first martyrdoms. By this time the friars had arrived, having taken ship with nominal Spanish forces from the Philippines. The pilot-major of the Spanish vessel, in an effort to impress Hideyoshi's attendants with the power of his king, remarked that Spain's successes with her conquistadors in the Americas were due largely to the undermining of the native culture by the missionaries. This coincided with what the bonzes had been telling Hideyoshi for years, and his reaction was swift. The Franciscans were sentenced to die at Nagasaki, and, after having been marched overland from Kyoto, they were crucified in the Japanese style. The Jesuits were exempted only because of Hideyoshi's need for the Portuguese trade. Put to death on February 5, 1597 (and now commemorated in the calendar of the saints, as are groups of later martyrs) were six Franciscans, seventeen of their Japanese assistants, and three Japanese Jesuit lay brothers who had been included by mistake.

During the next decade and a half the missionaries were able to recoup some of their losses, but Hideyoshi's successor, Ieyasu, discovered by 1614 that he no longer had need of the Jesuits. As the Dutch and some English were now visiting Japan, there were ships other than the *kurofune* on regular runs. There were also enough Japanese in Ieyasu's entourage who could speak Portuguese that the commercial role of the Jesuits was ended. Ieyasu became convinced, moreover, that the Portuguese would continue to trade even if the Jesuits were expelled. He needed only a pretense, which was given him when a Christian *daimyo* was caught in a court intrigue. The *daimyo* was executed, and Ieyasu was outraged that at the execution thousands of the *daimyo*'s subjects prayed aloud for him on their knees to the Christian God. This condescending to foreign ways by mere peasants was too much for him, and he issued the final expulsion edict, one swiftly carried out. Most of the missionaries left the country—although forty-seven European priests stayed behind in hiding—and the remaining churches were pulled down. At this time in Japan there were a quarter of a million Christians, in a population of twenty million, something like half again the ratio that prevails today if both Catholics and Protestants (who now outnumber the former) are counted. The vast majority went into quick apostasy. The priests who remained tried to disguise themselves as traders in order to travel about the countryside, but the authorities soon became aware of this and generally confined all Europeans, including the Dutch and English, to the greater Nagasaki area, where they could be watched. By the end of 1614 there were no more Christian *daimyos* in power, and there was no Christian who had the *shogun*'s ear.

The persecutions, though sporadic, were fierce. It is said that perhaps the friars had made a wiser choice than the Jesuits, since a higher proportion of peasants than *samurai* remained loyal to Christianity. In the early years the standard punishment for those who would not apostatize was burning. (Apostasy was signaled by stomping on an image, often of the Holy Family, known as a *fumie*.) An Englishman reported that he witnessed in Kyoto the execution of fifty-five people of all ages on the dry bed of the Kamo River in 1619. Little children were held amidst the flames by their mothers, who cried out, "Jesus receive their souls." Such scenes were repeated for a decade and a half, so that by 1630 Christianity seemed to be dead in Japan.

For the most stubborn there were other punishments. First there were the water tortures, but these were insufficiently gruesome; they were replaced by the pit. The victim was bound up to his shoulders like a mummy, with only one hand free to signal recantation, and was suspended by his feet in a pit partly filled with offal. Only the lower part of his legs would be above ground level. His forehead or temple was slit to let blood escape, thus easing the pressure and prolonging the torture. A recantation meant life; no recantation meant agonizing death. Most who did not recant lasted only a few hours. One girl lasted two weeks before dying. Those who apostatized and were released said the pain was unimaginable. The most famous apostate was old Christovao Ferreira, the Jesuit vice-provincial, who recanted after six hours in the pit in 1633. He lived for twenty years more, on occasion putting his signature to documents condemning the faith and helping the government ferret out hidden Christians; it is not known whether he rejected his apostasy before he died. In all, seven priests apostatized, only one a Japanese.

Christianity seemed dead, and Ieyasu's successors turned their attention elsewhere. Then came the Shimabara Rebellion in 1637. The immediate cause seemed to be the cruelty of a *daimyo*'s tax collectors, who tortured a man's daughter before his eyes in order to extract more money from him. The stewards were killed, but then the man was discovered to be a secret Christian. His neighbors and then the whole region rose in revolt in support of him, and by the time they captured the stronghold of Shimabara at least 37,000 had taken up arms. The *shogun* ordered troops to march against the fortress, but they suffered great casualties. The defenses were breached when the Dutch loaned the *shogun* heavy artillery, and all the rebels were killed. The last of the Portuguese traders then were expelled from nearby Nagasaki on the surmise that no rebellion could have occurred without their connivance.

Two years later the Portuguese sent a ship to Japan on a diplomatic mission, hoping to convince the *shogun* to reopen trade. Fortunately all members of the crew had confessed before the ship set sail, for they were executed as soon as they could be apprehended. There were other, smaller series of executions or persecutions in later years, as enclaves of Christians were discovered or as a few intrepid priests would slip into the country. In all roughly three thousand were killed for the faith; over seventy of them were Europeans.

It was not long before all attempts to send missionaries in secret were abandoned, since no one knew the language well enough to live for long even in disguise. The Church in Japan went into hiding. There remained a hierarchy of catechists who passed the faith from generation to generation. Cut off from all but two of the sacraments, the Christians suffered the accretion of certain superstitious practices and beliefs, but, when the next missionaries came in 1865, the Japanese Christians were able to recognize them by their veneration of Mary, their celibacy, and their loyalty to the pope. Like Lazarus, the Church in Japan was called back from the dead.